RATS

Rats

The Story of a Dog Soldier

by

Max Halstock

LONDON
VICTOR GOLLANCZ LTD
1981

© Max Halstock 1981

First published October 1981
Second impression November 1981

ISBN 0 575 03018 6

All photographs by Express Newspapers Ltd

Photoset by Rowland Phototypesetting Ltd
Bury St Edmunds, Suffolk
and printed in Great Britain by
St Edmundsbury Press, Bury St Edmunds, Suffolk

ONE

The voice of the Company Sergeant Major cracked like a whip across the parade ground. Immediately, and with that infinite precision only Her Majesty's Guards Division can achieve, the Prince of Wales' Company, First Battalion, the Welsh Guards, resplendent in black bearskins and scarlet tunics, snapped to attention. Not a man moved; not a man appeared to breathe. Time itself seemed to stop while they stood, immobile as toy soldiers, faces stiff and unyielding, muscles tight and controlled as though to sustain the charge of Napoleon's Old Guard.

Around the perimeter of this parade ground at the Guards' Depot at Pirbright in Surrey, wives and children of the guardsmen, with relatives and friends, waited in hushed expectancy, for this was no ordinary drill parade. This was a salute to an old soldier with a very special claim to loyalty and regard. As guardsmen and spectators waited, from the near distance, surrounded by an honour party of four guardsmen and accompanied by a personal escort, or ADC, the Retiring Member of the Regiment appeared. His gold campaign medal, a singular, indeed unique, award for Devotion to Duty, clinked softly under the chill April sun as he marched on to the parade ground. He appeared with a walk that contrasted with the sharp, measured paces of his escort. To be accurate, he seemed to roll a little with the characteristic gait which every man in the regiment had come to know with enormous affection; a gait that in others could have earned caustic comments from the sergeant major, and was described by his friends as 'more of a waddle than anything else'.

As his pace quickened and he began the long walk past the line of troops (it was noted thankfully that he moved with remarkable and commendable briskness and energy, having regard to his age and the state of his health), the Company Sergeant Major spoke again. At his command, short and sharp as the report of an M16 rifle, every right hand in the company was raised in salute.

A ripple of applause scattered from the civilian spectators. Television and Press cameras whirred and clicked. This was a moment to remember and it was right that it should be adequately and honourably recorded. Then, from the cloudless sky, a helicopter began to descend. As the roar of its engines and the beating of its rotors grew louder, everyone saw a dramatic—and entirely characteristic—change in the appearance of the Retiring Member.

The hairs on the back of his neck suddenly bristled, and his whole body stiffened in anticipation. For a moment, those in charge of the concourse looked on with carefully concealed alarm. Would the Retiring Member, who had been on sick leave for several weeks, still maintain enough remnants of discipline to complete the inspection as scheduled? Or would he, instead, make an undignified leap for the helicopter, piloted as it was (piloted in his special honour, indeed) by an old and dear friend from the campaign in South Armagh?

For a moment the issue hung in the balance. At a quiet word from the ADC, however, the Retiring Member regained his composure. The helicopter undoubtedly brought back recollections of other flights and memories of times past to him, as a song or a scent or the sound of laughter recalls other people and other places, but this was not the time or occasion for such recollections. He had not been awarded campaign medals to forget the seriousness of the parade. As though aware that the honour of the regiment, or at least its *amour propre*, was at stake, he had no intention, in these dying moments of his long and unusual career, of allowing personal feelings to eclipse his public *persona*. He was on parade as much as anyone else: the fact that the whole parade was in his honour only made him more aware and conscious of the need to maintain his dignity. His inspection continued without any outward sign of his innermost feelings.

The time now arrived for the Retiring Member to take his last salute and to bid farewell to old comrades. This was, by any standards, a deeply felt and poignant moment, and afterwards some guardsmen taking part were not above admitting that they had been close to tears—an experience widely admitted by others, not on parade, who had served with him and who watched the ceremony on television.

At a further command, the men drew themselves up in two lines facing each other and waited for the hovering helicopter to land. The Retiring Member, as everyone became aware, strained with impatience.

The helicopter was still a dozen or more feet off the ground when the ADC gave an almost imperceptible signal. At once, hands snapped up in salute again, and the Retiring Member, with not a glance to either side, began to amble towards the great machine. He still had several yards to go, when he broke into a sharp trot.

The aircraft was still six feet from touchdown when the Retiring Member, caution cast to the winds as had always been his habit and disregarding the state of his health, launched himself spectacularly into space.

His old comrades waited to see whether age and wounds had lost him any of his almost uncanny skill and surefootedness. Not so. They heaved a collective (and silent) sigh of relief as he scrambled aboard successfully, although for a second it seemed that he might slip. A warm burst of cheering and of renewed applause came from the civilian onlookers as the helicopter, its engines revving fiercely, rose slowly into the air and lazily swung away. Moments later, it became a dwindling speck in the distance, and the British Army had seen the last of one of its most remarkable and best-loved recruits.

The Retiring Member was unusual in other ways. He soldiered on four feet and not on two; he had a perky tail and floppy ears and a bark to match his bite. He was the celebrated dog-soldier, Rats, off to begin what everybody on that parade—and thousands more in countries as far apart as Germany and France, the United States of America and Canada—sincerely hoped would be a long and happy retirement.

He went in the knowledge—and if this seems far-fetched, most of his friends will swear that he was the kind of dog that understood this sort of thing—that he had served longer in one of the world's most troublesome and dangerous spots than any other individual British soldier, and he bore with him more than his fair share of battle scars.

8

He had been shot at more times than anybody could count—when he retired a shotgun pellet was still lodged in the loose flesh along his chest. He had been blown up by a bomb; four pieces of metal still lay trapped along his spine. He had been wounded by an exploding firebomb, which had burnt away several inches of his tail, leaving him with only a short stub. He had been run over twice by vehicles in the course of his duties—leaving him with permanently bent paws and a healed broken leg. And he had been stabbed, or otherwise wounded, by a sharp instrument, which left a perceptible gash in his stomach. Besides that, Rats had suffered an impressive catalogue of bites incurred during the course of fending off much larger, fiercer dogs whose masters set them to this task with the intention of harassing army patrols.

None of this, of course, can completely explain why so many people had gathered to bid so ceremonial a farewell to a dog. This was by no means the usual way of a canine goodbye, but then Rats was not the usual sort of regimental dog. His arrival, his attachment to various fighting units, and in particular his love of flying by helicopter had become a part of British Army folklore. The origins and upbringing of Rats, even the source or sources of his name (and ought it, indeed, to be Rats at all?) are shielded by an impenetrable veil of time and myth. This is not unfitting, of course, for a native of Ireland, a land that is the home and scene of the oldest legends and the most ancient mythical poetry in all northern Europe.

Some might even see Rats as a curious reincarnation of those war-dogs and great hounds, another Bran or Skolawn, perhaps, which feature so vividly in the epic pages of old Irish legends.

Odd, Rats certainly was. To suggest that he had some pedigree would give a Cruft's judge apoplexy. A corporal in the Queen's Own Highlanders, who knew Rats better than most men, feels convinced that he had a great deal of the alsatian in him. Others found traces of everything from Portuguese water-spaniels to Patagonian pie-dogs. The consensus, however, is that the predominant strains were corgi and Jack Russell terrier. Whatever other dogs feature in his pedigree, they combined to give Rats ample courage, a remarkable, sometimes uncanny intelligence, and an unshakeable conviction that he had been put on earth to dominate all dogs twice his size and over.

In dealing with a dog that, in so many senses, has become surrounded by the hallmarks of legend and folklore, the fundamental questions of his life, such as where he came from, who saw him first, and which detachment of the British armed forces serving in Crossmaglen first enrolled him on their strength, become potentially controversial issues and are best left shrouded in the mists of Celtic conjecture.

Certain detachments of the British army, for instance, in pursuit of a claim that he first became attached to them, have gone so far as to produce photographic evidence purporting to show a dog identifiable as Rats with one of their soldiers. Others claim that such pictures, although interesting, lack credibility. That dogs are clearly to be seen in the photographs no one can deny; but while a dog is a dog, that dog is not necessarily Rats; and no other individual dog answers with complete satisfaction to his description.

In one photograph, a dog appears with ears similar to Rats', but there any similarity ends. In another, the hindquarters look alike; in a third, the paws. But the searcher after truth in this matter is left with the feeling that Rats' genealogy, like so much else in Celtic lands, cannot be properly established.

Certainly, when a detachment of the Black Watch was stationed in Crossmaglen for part of 1975 and throughout the whole of 1976, and when 'A' Company, Royal Highland Fusiliers had a spell over the New Year in 1976, no animal even faintly answering to the celebrated dog's description was in residence. A Fusilier major, indeed, is prepared to go on record as doubting the advisability of allowing *any* such dog on their premises. Even if so permitted, he saw disadvantages in allowing a dog to accompany patrols in what has come to be known as 'bandit country'. He was by no means implying that he held to a dogma in this matter; merely that he felt it was allowable to have reservations.

What, for instance, would happen if the dog barked at the wrong time? Here the false from the true dog-soldiers could swiftly be divided. Rats *never* barked at the wrong time. He had a superbly developed military instinct, and no one associated with him recalled him barking unless to help confound the Queen's enemies. But to make assurance doubly sure, a couple of Guards officers recall that 'Rats was never permitted to go out on anything remotely approaching a covert operation, where a stealthy approach might be necessary''.

There is no known instance where Rats, silent or not, ever endangered any patrol. On the contrary, in conditions which we will examine in greater detail later, it has been claimed that his presence was often of the greatest assistance to the men who had befriended him. At least one NCO, it would seem, almost certainly owes his life to Rats' signal of recognition.

Whatever the reasons (most of his friends hold to the opinion that Rats himself had yet to decide on a military career) the first four or five years of his life are a complete blank so far as the army's records are concerned. Then, early in 1978, 42 Commando, Royal Marines, found themselves ensconced in the service base at Crossmaglen, County Armagh.

The base is a relatively narrow building containing offices, cookhouse, living accommodation with bunk beds for all and the various other items which make life bearable in an enclosed and protected area. The base adjoins the old local police station which is surrounded by screens of corrugated iron surmounted by barbed wire and contains a helipad. A new police station was opened in August 1980 and is completely separate from the base.

When a patrol from 42 Commando first saw Rats he looked much like any other mongrel pup, not particularly pleasing and with nothing to distinguish him from dozens of other stray or ownerless dogs in this part of Ireland. The word 'pup' is used advisedly, for throughout much of his military career his comrades lived in the firm conviction that Rats was little more than a baby. It was not until his general health deteriorated to such a degree that his retirement from the army was recommended, or rather insisted upon by an army veterinary surgeon, that the truth emerged about his age. It appears that he must have been born in 1972 or 1973 and was, therefore, in his terms (taking seven years in a dog's life as being equal to one year for a human being) reasonably mature. What tended to fool his new-found friends was his sheer perkiness. He

12

had not advanced in any way towards the sobriety of middle age, and was as eager and ready for fun and excitement as any young soldier.

The first authenticated sighting of Rats was on a piece of waste ground adjoining a small housing estate called Ardross (The High Wood) on the western outskirts of Crossmaglen. Rats seemingly was in residence on this piece of ground and apparently living off it, although exactly off what has never been ascertained. The town, in fact, had an excellent complement of strays, a miscellany of breeds, cross-breeds and half-breeds that, whatever else their condition, were obviously well fed. This is only one of the notable aspects of Crossmaglen, a town whose inhabitants hold the usual rural attitude towards dogs: that they are only worth having around the place as working animals or sporting animals. The urban concept of dogs as pets was as foreign to most of them as these bustling young men in their berets, green fatigues, rifles and other weapons speaking dialects of England, Scotland and Wales that were often almost as unintelligible to the locals as Urdu.

Nevertheless, as befits a place with a weekly cattle market (every Friday) and plenty of country produce, few of the strays appeared to suffer any signs of emaciation or malnutrition. Rats' subsequent actions, therefore, were unlikely to have been dictated by hunger, but more likely by another almost equally basic instinct which, apart from the natural responses of kindness and friendship offered by the troops, dates back many millennia. It is the strange and strong relationship between dogs and men, the wish to go soldiering with humans, to find friends with those who follow the drum.

No food or other inducement was offered by the Marine

patrol. The first friendly approaches came from Rats. Report has it that Rats came bounding up to the patrol, tail wagging furiously, and made one or two playful assaults on their bootlaces. As this occurred at a time when gestures of friendship or of an even less than glacial warmth were non-existent so far as the locals were concerned, the commando response was predictable. Rats received the soft side of the boot to start with, but this soon gave way to pats on the head and approving calls of 'Good dog'. In an area where the unseen but deadly enemy could lurk round every corner, every tree and bush and at the other side of every hedgerow, the behaviour of this small dog was a welcome intervention.

The question as to why Rats should personally have emerged as 'the soldier's friend', rather than any of a dozen or more strays scampering around Crossmaglen, has much to do with his lovability and his loyalty. His eyes were more appealing, his waddle more charming. But, over and above everything else, was his attitude. Once the daily patrols had begun to notice him and respond to his eager greetings, he appeared to adopt them before they adopted him. This process on his part consisted of displaying a fierce possessiveness. Once Rats had led the way, the whole pack of Crossmaglen strays attempted to join him and all wished to show that they were also 'soldiers' friends'.

Rats, as though sensing the threat to his starring role, immediately showed that this was not for them. Some might be called; only he was chosen. He would, according to the Marines, 'not let any other dog come near us'. Growling or barking or making fierce rushes, he drove off the pack. Welcome as his friendliness was, it is doubtful if things would have gone as far as they did if Rats had not decided to make himself a useful member of the patrols.

The first sign the Marines had that Rats could play a military role was when he began to warn them of the approach of strangers by growling softly. Given that a dog's hearing and instincts are generally more fully developed than those of a man, his presence with a patrol proved almost as useful as a mobile radar scanner. Rats now found himself not just a soldiers' friend; he became a dog soldier.

Inquiries having established that he did not belong to anybody, he was allowed inside the gates of the base. An army blanket was put down on the floor of the Briefing Room and he immediately took up residence. At this stage in relationships, no attempt was made, either by the Marines or Rats, to establish any of the strong personal ties between individual soldiers and the dog that later developed. The whole Commando unit took it upon themselves to be responsible, in turn, for his welfare and comfort, making sure, in particular, that he was fed and watered and kept as clean as possible.

Marine recollections of these early days show that he had yet to develop a passion for helicopters which later became such a mark of his military service. But that he had a passion for riding in military vehicles was evident from the start.

The focus of his attention became Saracen armoured cars, familiar to anybody who has watched TV news items from Northern Ireland. Rats, according to the Marines, seized on every possible opportunity to climb into one, and the sound of an engine starting up was 'enough to make him dash out and jump in the back'. Whenever he had the chance he climbed in, curled up – and promptly went to sleep.

By all accounts it was an agreeable life so far as Rats was concerned. He enjoyed the best of food, constant attention and comradeship, a sense of adventure during army patrols, the 'luxury' of bouncing about in a 'Sarrycan' and of being the most important dog in town.

But Crossmaglen, for all its apparent sleepiness and remoteness, has not been for more than a decade a resort where people go for their health. It lies in the front-line of a strange but ever dangerous battlefield. Soon, Rats was to discover that when you follow the drum, all is not pageantry; or in his case, lavish steaks, the warmth of gas fires or the excitement of patrols and armoured cars. With dramatic suddenness, he was to learn that the loyalty and affection he had given to the armed services could involve him in far more serious and agonising matters.

TWO

That morning, everyone in the patrol appeared to be slightly tense—except for one member, who trotted along perkily on four legs.

In theory, every patrol should always have felt tense, but in practice patrols were a welcome if unusual and often dangerous relief from boredom and waiting.

Young men, cooped up in camp at Crossmaglen pondering their eventual chances against a booby-trapped vehicle or some other IRA explosive device operated by remote control, or maybe wondering why they were living like latter-day troglodytes, or perhaps instead thinking of their girlfriends or wives and families miles away, often welcomed the sheer physical exercise of a patrol. Above all, they needed its purposeful nature; they felt they were doing something positive, not simply waiting in a passive way.

As a Guards NCO has explained it, 'Off duty, you couldn't go outside the camp, really, so the men had to live a very contained sort of life. You could go out along the perimeter of the camp, but that was very small. And all the time you had to be careful. The tension was there continually, in a sense, but it would diminish immediately you went on patrol, for then everything became physical. We used to try and make the patrols as strenuous as possible to try and relieve the tension. If we didn't patrol, it would be traumatic, claustrophobic. You'd feel you almost needed a psychiatrist . . .'

To soldiers who had, in some instances, already served for ten years in the army, who had been trained to a pitch of physical perfection and skill with weapons and who had never experienced what they called *real* soldiering, patrolling the lanes in and around the Crossmaglen area or farther out into the South Armagh countryside was a godsend. At last they felt that they were doing the job for which they had been trained; finally they could experience for themselves the proof, the evidence, that the army's role was a vital one. This was not make-believe, a war game or manoeuvres; this was real.

The risk was real, too; the tight, held-in risk that a bullet or bomb would suddenly end your life, or worse—though this was a deeply hidden and only rarely expressed fear— that it might leave you not killed but blinded or paralysed, perhaps a cripple for the rest of your days.

But when one became a soldier these risks were accepted with the heightened feeling of a challenge. They were almost a trial that in a strange way, and possibly inexplicable to a civilian, you almost felt anxious to face. The challenge was to one's manhood and one's ability to survive the worst. Young men wanted to know, deep inside themselves, how they would react, how they would acquit themselves, when sudden deadly danger faced them. This would be the supreme test of their training and their calling; to surmount it would be the mark of the warrior.

All, of course, felt a calm confidence in themselves, and in their training. They knew that, whenever a crisis arose, the first essential was to identify its source and then to deal with it as calmly as they could, using all the expertise at their command. Once a man realised this, soldiering became a job, almost, but never quite, like any other.

The secret was to divest this job of a paralysing element of danger; always to be alert to its proximity, but not to allow the knowledge to prevent one's capacity to act. This was where training came in; it prepared men psychologically as well as physically.

This particular patrol felt tense as distinct from being just acutely alert, because this was the beginning of a hand-over period, so to half its members the patrol was new and unfamiliar, over strange and dangerous ground. Crossmaglen had similarities with serving in trench warfare in a front-line position in the Great War. Troops could not be exposed to such a contained existence for very long, and therefore regimental companies worked on a rotating basis. Northern Ireland duty for the British Army as a whole was organised along these lines.

Companies were expected, on average, to spend about four months in Crossmaglen. They would then hand over to an incoming regiment. A fortnight or ten days before, or in the case of company commanders or other senior officers, perhaps a little longer, the newcomers would begin to arrive. The company commander, of course, would already have spent four or five days in the area, perhaps two or three months earlier, getting to know the district and the general problems, and finding out how the regiment he was to relieve handled things. A week or so before the actual hand-over, which was a *working* hand-over, section commanders moved in to familiarise themselves with the operations.

Afterwards, in a short two-hour period, while everything inside the camp continued to work smoothly and patrols went in and out in the normal way, the full handover took place. A helicopter would air-lift eight men at a time of the incoming regiment into the base, and take eight men out, repeating the exercise until the handover was complete. The whole operation was quick and efficient.

For most of the newcomers, even though hardened to nondescript accommodation as part of their training, the base that was to be their home for the next few months had hardly the air of a 'desirable residence'.

In the patrol on this October day in 1978 were two Grenadier Guards NCOs of the 2nd Company, 1st Battalion, members of the advance party who had arrived a week before the rest, and two Marines from 42 Commando, Royal Marines. The Guards were preparing to take over from the Marines. The Grenadiers were Lance-Corporal Kevin Kinton, son of a coalminer, who had been born in the little mining village of Calverton, outside Nottingham, and who was then aged 18, and Lance-Sergeant Keith Regan, aged 28, from Worcester, and son of a lorry-driver.

Probably neither would have considered himself typical of the army intake in the Sixties and Seventies. It is only when one looks carefully at the individual motives men have for joining the army, that one realises that no one *is* typical; each man has his own reasons, as individual as he is himself.

Lance-Corporal (now Sergeant) Kinton had joined up when he was only sixteen. All his family on the male side had been coalminers, and he himself expected to go down the pit, but his father, a coalface worker, was against the idea.

'There's no way you're going down, so far as I'm concerned,' he had declared firmly. Kinton, therefore, had looked at other careers. He briefly tried a part-time job in a garage, repairing motor-cycles, but then decided that he would join the Royal Marines. He was good at sport and enjoyed the outdoor life. He played hockey for his school, was a strong cross-country runner and a useful cricketer, and had won a county trial for both hockey and cross-country.

He hoped that he might become a swimming canoeist, but when he attended a Royal Marine selection board, there were no vacancies for canoeists, swimming or otherwise, therefore he decided to join the army. What he did not want was to be what he considered 'an average soldier', and his ambition was the Guards Independent Parachute Company. By the time he had finished training, however, the paras had been disbanded.

In Crossmaglen, Kinton was a 'brick' commander (a 'brick' is the nickname for a unit of four men) and this was his first tour in Northern Ireland. He had served in Hong Kong, attended a tactics course in Brunei, and had also done a tour with the Battalion in Jamaica. He did not feel in the least worried when the helicopter first flew in over Crossmaglen bringing him in to the base.

'In fact,' he says now, 'it was really exciting—actually doing something for which I had trained so long.'

When he saw Crossmaglen, he could not believe that this small town could be the source of so many stories about danger that he had heard from others who had served there.

'I thought, none of this stuff could happen here—it's only a small peaceful village.'

As they whirled in to the touchdown, he saw Marines standing anxiously near the helipad waiting to come out. Then it was one man in, one man out and Kevin Kinton found himself jumping down from the helicopter and clumping heavily into the base at a run in full kit.

It was about eight o'clock in the evening when they arrived and within seconds he was inside this vaguely steamy room, and somebody was saying, 'Dump your kit—and there's your bunk.' Then it was round to Stores to draw a flak jacket and boots and battle kit, to be ready for action.

Kinton had, in fact, noticed two dogs also waiting by the helipad when he had come down, but paid little attention to them. Later, the smaller corgi-type was to be named Rat—in the singular then, not the plural as Rats later came to be called—and his companion, a big black Labrador, known as Fleabus.

Fleabus was given this name because 'he was a big and really dirty dog'. In fact, owing to the climatic conditions, Crossmaglen was one of the wettest and muddiest camps the Battalion could recall.

'There was mud everywhere. You were constantly up to your knees in it, and Fleabus was always dirty, really filthy and covered in mud. Rat was a different kettle of fish altogether, much more intelligent. That was the first point about him—he was *really* intelligent. He used his brains, did Rat, and bounced around and avoided the mud.'

On the first occasion both dogs had appeared well-trained and used to army life. Neither barked or showed any excitement when the helicopter landed. They just stood there, watching, ears pricked. But even then, Rat had appeared to be the leader—quicker, more alert, and much faster-thinking.

There had been little time for any discussion before Kevin Kinton was marching out through the big corrugated-iron gate and having his first close-up view of Crossmaglen.

From the air, there had been no opportunity to do anything more than to guess at its size. On the ground now, on this cold night, he could see the damage.

'The moment you came out of the camp, the first thing you saw were the splatter marks of bullets all round the place. You find these marks all round the town and a lot obviously caused by bombs.'

Crossmaglen has a total population of 1,085 people, 532 males, and 553 females—which would not make a very big crowd at a football match. Crossmaglen is strongly Republican and Catholic, and the only building likely to catch the eye is the church of St Patrick.

Crossmaglen possesses two schools, both called St Joseph's—a secondary and a primary school. It also has thirteen public houses. This, of course, is far from being an Irish record; Milton Mallbay in County Clare has 27 to serve a population of only 650 people, but 13 for 1,085 inhabitants is still a large number.

Crossmaglen has a very impressive market square, reputedly one of the largest in Ireland. The population of Ireland, relative to England's, is tiny, so that Irish people have always enjoyed plenty of room to move. There is rarely any sense of crowding and many small Irish towns, therefore, boast huge squares. On market days, when farmers and their carts, cars and cattle crowd in, they seem by no means too big.

The square has two memorials. The first is the Republican monument, a partly-abstract, partly-representational work in stone of a human figure, struggling agonisingly to rise from the clutches of a bird thought to be a phoenix. In Gaelic lettering, an inscription records the glory that is due to men who have 'died for an unselfish love of Irish freedom'.

Not far away stands another monument to events in this little town over the past decade. This is known as the Baruckie Sanger. Sanger is army jargon for a Protected Observation Post, and Baruckie commemorates the name of the unfortunate British paratrooper who died at this spot when the IRA bombed it—and almost, it is said, killed Rats in the process. A further reminder of this bloody incident is a splattered hole in a nearby wall which also suffered in the blast.

If any tourist brochure were issued on behalf of Crossmaglen—and there is none—it would probably omit such details, and although the little town suffers from the blight which afflicts most of Ireland—too much rain—it could, in normal times, possibly make out a case for a visit. Nearby runs the River Fane, which is reputed to be well-stocked with trout and salmon. There are other good fishing waters at Lough Ross, and an historic castle at Glasdrumman, with prehistoric remains within a mile or so. Traditionally, the area surrounding the town has been famous for a particularly delicate and beautiful lace called Carrickmacross lace. The fields support fine herds of cattle, among which, when out on patrol, Rats would delight in scampering, and the sight of him attempting to order the cattle about is one that no soldier who saw him will easily forget. The cows, it should be said, rarely welcomed his attentions, and on at least one occasion, a cow turned, lowered its horns and charged Rats, who immediately retreated.

Of much more significance to the British troops stationed there is the fact that 'the Border' lies only one and a half miles to the south. The Border, of course, is the line that marks off the six counties of Northern Ireland from the twenty-six that make up the Republic. In more senses than one, Crossmaglen is a frontier town. For long it has been a great centre of smuggling—and even now, some of the resentment or sullenness shown towards British troops is not entirely political but has to do with their interference to this lucrative trade.

If, in the 1920s when the Border had been drawn, it had been agreed on a strictly Catholic–Protestant basis, South Down, South Armagh, all of Tyrone and Fermanagh and the city of Londonderry would most likely have been handed to the South. The North in return would have gained small areas in Donegal and Monaghan. Had the Border, in short, been drawn according to the wishes of the local inhabitants, Crossmaglen would now lie in what is called the Republic of Ireland—and Rats would probably never have become a soldiers' friend in the British army.

For Kevin Kinton, that first night seemed very quiet. The army had closed the town for an Op Tonnage—the name given to an operation to bring in building and other kit from Belfast, using heavy lorries. All roads had to be secured when the lorries travelled. Vehicle Check Points, known as VCPs, had been set up in Crossmaglen and along the approach road. The troops were kept busy, stopping and checking cars or other vehicles, and Kinton felt keenly interested in the job.

'You had this feeling that you were doing a real job,' he says. 'And because the whole town was closed down, I didn't worry—I felt a certain sense of security. I know I shouldn't have allowed myself to feel like this—but you do sort of relax a bit.'

What he remembers most, in fact, is that it was 'freezing cold' and the roads were covered in frost. But every ten minutes a Saracen armoured car came along, and they were able to jump briefly into the back and have a cup of tea. After two hours or so, his duty period was over, and he remembers thinking, 'Well, this isn't as hard as I thought it would be—*and* for my first time out in Ireland.'

From the start, he had been keyed up in the expectation of trouble, and he could almost feel the adrenalin draining away as he walked back to camp. Inside, it was straight into the off-duty routine that was to mark his tour: into his bunk and off to sleep.

He was awakened after two hours and went out again to continue checking vehicles, for the lorries were still rumbling down from Belfast. A VCP had been set up opposite the Crossmaglen piggeries, and a Sarrycan was parked nearby.

On one side of the road, beside this checkpoint, was a derelict house, and on the other side, a telegraph pole, alongside the piggeries' wall. Everything went smoothly, and when Kevin Kinton left to go back to camp again, the Sarrycan was still parked, a haven of hot cups of tea for the troops, a dark, welcome and protective shape. So the night passed; two hours on duty, two hours off. In the morning the patrol set out.

26

The Marine brick-commander, from whom Kinton was taking over, had been waiting in the Briefing Room, next to the Ops Room; and on instructions from the Company Commander, Major Charles Woodrow, MC, QGM, Kinton went to see him.

'I'll give you a quick briefing now,' the Marine told him, 'and then brief you further while you're walking round.'

Outside, most of the barriers had been removed and Crossmaglen was back to normal—which in army language meant that it was highly hostile and equally dangerous. The patrol, accompanied by the little dog Rat, moved up the town to St Patrick's church, and the Marine brick-commander showed Kinton and his fellow Grenadier the graveyard, and favourite places from which the IRA sometimes sniped at the Baruckie Sanger. Then he led them down a road where, on earlier tours, soldiers had been killed, and to other danger spots in the town, including sites near the schools from which the IRA had previously opened fire.

At that hour, the children were still in their classrooms although due soon for their morning break. After the patrol had spent a little time reconnoitring the position, it moved off. Back up the road, the Grenadiers were trying to accustom themselves to the realisation that this peaceful scene, seemingly the parallel many remembered from schooldays in their own home towns and villages, was actually a total delusion and that at any moment firing against them could begin.

This idea seemed impossible, almost ludicrous to Kinton—why, there was even that corgi-like dog he had dimly noticed the previous night strutting ahead at the Marine brick-commander's heels, as though out for a walk with his master. How could danger and death possibly be equated with such a homely, familiar sight?

Keith Regan's duties at Crossmaglen were, in the event, to be largely of a non-combatant type. He was a Company medic, and although like every man on the base he had to be prepared to use weapons, his role was essentially that of bringing medical aid to any wounded man—and for his courage and resource in this capacity he was later to be awarded the BEM.

As the tour progressed, he was to find himself frequently cooped up in the medical hut but, like the rest of the Company, he went out on patrol occasionally and liked to do so. Now he was familiarising himself with the countryside, marking the terrain and its features for the time when he might be called out to render medical assistance under fire.

As the patrol moved along the road towards the piggeries, it contacted another patrol, again consisting of two Marines and two Grenadiers. Heading this 'brick' was Platoon Sergeant Michael Knight from Maidstone, also aged 28, who had been in the army since he was fifteen.

On his father's side, Knight came from an old army family who had seen service as far back as the Zulu War. As his patrol handed over the area to Sergeant Regan's patrol and moved off to another part of the town, Knight noticed the corgi cross-breed strutting about with Regan's patrol. Although only newly arrived in Crossmaglen, he had plenty of reason to notice the dog. As it was the start of a hand-over period the base was lamentably overcrowded and, indeed, he had been forced to bunk in a garden shed because Marines were still in occupation of the main accommodation. He had quickly noticed what he later described as 'this scruffy, dirty little dog, always getting in the way of troops moving around', and became even more aware of it when it suddenly ran under his feet and tripped him up.

As he remembers the incident, he had 'a few well-chosen words to say to that dog', before going on with his duties.

As Kinton's patrol carefully approached the piggeries, the Marines advised him to walk on the left-hand side of the road, near the derelict house where he had spent most of the previous night at the VCP. Although the army took care to avoid derelict houses while on patrol this particular house had been checked before the VCP had been set up, and indeed, the Sarrycan, which had been parked there throughout Op Tonnage, had moved away only an hour or so earlier. By any reasonable standards, this hardly gave the IRA time to move in and plant an explosive device.

Much more dangerous, it seemed, was the potential threat from the area near the telegraph pole. Here they could see the marks of fresh diggings at the foot of the pole. These looked menacing and it seemed better to give them a clear berth. A mine could easily be concealed only inches beneath the surface of the soil. In the light of what happened next. the calibre and ingenuity of 'the Opposition' (as the army labels the IRA) was seen at its most callous. As Sergeant Kinton recalls, 'Those diggings were *meant* to force us near the derelict house, to take the left-hand side of the road.'

As he began to walk past the stone entrance posts to the house it suddenly occurred to him that everything seemed

29

too quiet. He does not know whether this was some kind of premonition of danger but abruptly, in that instant of utter silence, the bomb exploded.

He learned later that explosives had been hidden inside two Calor gas containers planted behind the stone posts and that they had been detonated by radio control, possibly by someone watching the patrol who waited until they were actually opposite the gate posts and then sent the activating signal. Or maybe the watcher gave a sign to the controller who could be far away, over the border.

This bomb was to change Kevin Kinton's attitude towards life—other people's and his own. For the first time, he realised, there were human beings whom he had never seen, who had probably never seen him, but who still wished to kill him.

'The act of somebody trying to kill you makes you think differently. I now realised that the world outside was often a vile and vicious place, that people are *out* to do you down. This left me with real mental scars. Suddenly, life seemed cheap.'

He still does not believe he can ever again look upon his fellow human beings in the way he had been brought up to do before this experience.

At the time, however, he did not realise what was happening to him.

'It felt as though somebody had jumped from a window and landed on my back. Thinking that somebody had actually jumped on me, I tried to swing round to push him off.'

But Kinton discovered that he couldn't move, that his breath had been blown from his body with the force of the blast, and in his words, 'everything was just all black'.

30

He felt his eyes burning and a fierce sensation of heat, as though somebody had opened the door of a scorching hot oven in his face.

Then he had the strange sensation that time itself was stopping, or rather, slowing; winding down and down, as he had seen in films like *The Wild Bunch*, where the camera slowed the action when horse-riders were shot by machine guns. Noises echoed through his head as though from a vast distance.

The next thing he knew, he realised that he was lying on the ground and everything was speeding up again to normal. He felt no pain at this stage, just a struggle to get his breath back. That was the moment that he realised that somebody had attempted to kill him.

He looked around. Black debris like giant flakes of soot, with black tiles from the derelict house and pieces of wood, appeared to be hanging in the air above him and now about to fall. Kinton scrambled to his feet and dived towards the nearest shelter, a doorway in a range of terrace houses about thirty metres away. Instinctively, he tried to get as far from the bomb blast as possible, and flung himself into the second doorway rather than the first. As he huddled there, he felt strangely cheerful.

'Somebody,' he thought, 'has tried to kill me—and *they haven't succeeded*!' This realisation elated him. When the Marine brick-commander came down—'and he was in a bit of a shock'—and asked: 'What—happened here?' Kinton seemed almost euphoric.

'Somebody's tried to kill me,' he explained. 'But they haven't succeeded.'

Then with the soot and debris still falling down, he and the Marine realised that somebody had not been so fortunate. They could hear a man screaming and, as Kinton tried to sort things out in his mind, the sound of a stricken dog yelping. Neither he nor the Marine however could see anything, for a great dark cloud still obscured the sky and everything around them.

A few yards away, Sergeant Regan, blown over by the blast, was picking himself up. He was spared the screams and the dog's yelping for the explosion had momentarily deafened him. Then, as the smoke and dirt cleared away and he saw a wounded Marine on the ground he snapped into action. With the help of Kinton and the Marine 'brick', they did their best to patch up the man's wounds and swathed them in field-dressings. At the same time, they radioed for help. Within minutes, a helicopter landed in a field beside the road and the Quick Reaction Force led by the Company Comander, Major Woodrow, jumped out. Units of the local police force also arrived, and within seconds the wounded Marine was airborne to hospital, where, despite the speed with which he had been moved, he died three days later.

At this stage, there was no sign of the corgi-like dog that had accompanied the patrol and which would soon be known to the Grenadiers generally as 'Rat'. Not that anybody had much thought for any dog. The time had not yet come when the health and well-being of 'Rat' would seem almost as important to some of the soldiers as their own survival.

He still had to make his way into the affections of the British army, to become for hard-pressed men a focus of all that seemed kind and humane and loving and compassionate in life. In that moment of reaction, it was a time only for the steeling of hearts, for a recognition that this must be the strangest and most treacherous of all wars.

In the near distance, the school bell clanged and the playground was, suddenly and incongruously, filled with chattering, cheerful children.

THREE

After this incident, and when Corporal Kinton had been sent back to camp in a Sarrycan, Major Woodrow began to walk to the camp himself, scanning the surrounding countryside for any signs or clues to the bombers. In a short while, he came across a trail of blood in the road that apparently led from a field. He followed this, half expecting that it would lead him to some badly wounded person; instead, to his surprise, it led straight back to base.

When he returned to the base his immediate thought was for Regan and Kinton.

'You have to be careful after a bomb explosion,' he explains. 'People suffer a certain degree of shock, and do things they don't normally do. So I was just checking that we hadn't got somebody wandering around with a whacking great wound in him—that was why I had followed the blood trail.'

In fact, Corporal Kinton was more seriously injured than he had realised. He felt something trickling down the back of his neck and imagined it was sweat. When he wiped it away with his hand, however, he found that it was blood. Then his legs began to shake uncontrollably and two hours later, the helicopter was landing him at Musgrave Hospital in Belfast, where he was to spend the next five days.

On his return, he hoped to go straight out on patrol

34

again. Major Woodrow protested gently. 'Seeing you've had such a bad introduction,' he said, 'I think we can let you sit this one out.' But Kinton insisted that he had to go out again at once.

When it became clear that neither Regan nor Kinton were responsible for the trail of blood, it occurred to Major Woodrow that perhaps one of the dogs that hung around outside the camp, or one of the two or three allowed inside it, might have been hurt. As dogs were low on his list of priorities, though, and there was much to do following such a serious incident, he dismissed the thought for the time being.

A day or so later, still mildly puzzled as to the source of the blood trail, he came across the little corgi cross-breed in the medical hut, where it was being attended to. The dog had been caught up in the blast and had been badly cut about and wounded and was the obvious source of the blood trail. After the blast it had apparently gone missing for a day or two before creeping back into the camp. Major Woodrow is a lover of dogs, and the owner of a basset hound called Willoughby, so he patted the little dog on the head and after 'encouraging the medics to get on with it' moved on to other, more pressing problems.

'The important thing', he remembers, 'was that if the dog were already attached to the base, then it should be attended to. Indeed, in the circumstances, we'd have done the same thing whether it belonged to us or not. And, of course, it didn't matter whether it was a human that had been hurt or an animal. You have to remember that soldiers have a strong affinity for children and dogs. We don't ignore dogs.'

At the time, of course, he was not certain whether the

35

dog had been 'taken on the strength' but for some reason still felt mildly interested in the animal—perhaps because it so clearly had character.

The son of a major-general, Charles Woodrow had been educated at Wellington and Sandhurst, joined the Grenadier Guards in 1965, and was now on his seventh tour in Northern Ireland. Before this particular tour he had been staff officer at Brigade HQ and on visits to Crossmaglen had seen this dog, or one very like it, hanging around the base with other dogs. Of course, there were always dogs patrolling outside the gates of any army post, and to this day he does not know whether or not Rat had become a permanent member of the garrison at this early stage. He inclines to think that he had not. But afterwards the Marines confirmed that they had found him in the town, and that when he insisted on following them through the gates they had 'adopted' him. So far as Major Woodrow was concerned, he was happy to have the dog on the base.

'Soldiers like having a dog—that's the first thing.' And there was another reason: 'This rather unpleasant business, that they are a good way of triggering a device. I would rather lose a dog than a soldier—if I have to lose anything or anyone.'

The wounded Rat, in fact, had been found inside the base perimeter by Lance-Sergeant Tim Fielding, at 27 a veteran of almost ten years' army service and a freefall parachuting, a skiing and a mountaineering enthusiast.

'When I first saw Rat he had a hole in his side,' he says. Both his ears had also been cut. Fielding was fond of dogs and owned one of his own, called Gunner. He lifted up the cross-breed and carried him gently into the medical hut where Sergeant Regan helped to 'sew him up' and bind his wounds and generally give him medical care.

The little dog, however, which had just managed to crawl into the camp, languished for the next four days, lying either curled up in the medical hut or dozing quietly on top of one of the three-tier bunks in the big eighteen-man dormitory. He went completely off his food and lost weight. Fielding quickly became extremely attached to the little dog. He was rusty brown and white in colouring and in good health should weigh about 11 pounds. Tim Fielding more or less personally adopted the dog and was compelled to forcefeed him in order to save his life. After about a week, Rat began to show signs of reviving.

In one sense, this proved an unwelcome development. Rat started to pick at his food again, eating while he sat beside one of the bunks or even moving into the mess room. Then, to everyone's horror, he started to amble off on his own into the Company Commander's room, where there was a single bunk, and proceeded to have a quick 'pee' on top of his bed.

Today, Major Woodrow recalls this with a smile.

'I'm sure we called him Rat because he was so scraggy and so revolting,' he says. 'I mean, he was really an unpleasant-looking little chap at that stage—dirty and smelly certainly. And probably with fleas—though I don't know. Anyhow, he was *revolting*. Bright and cheerful certainly, but with these absolutely revolting habits. He used to pee all over the Officers' Mess and then be sick in the Officers' Mess too. That's how I remember him—always being sick in the Mess. And then he used to sleep on top of my bed—or sometimes under it. How did I like it? Well, I've been used to dogs at home all my life, so I wasn't really fussed.'

This, then, in the formal sense appears to have been the start of Rat's real relationship with the British army. In due course he was given a name which seems partly to have derived from 'rations' (because the Company had by now begun to make itself responsible for his food) and partly, as Major Woodrow recalls it, because he 'vaguely looked like a rat'. And partly, too, perhaps, because, when he regained his health and vigour, he would chase rats. In due course, indeed, a rat bit him—adding to his list of wounds received on active service.

At this stage, the dog Fleabus was also in the camp, and at least one other dog was scurrying about the camp.

'But Rat soon became the most prominent,' says Major Woodrow. 'I think, indeed, he became the outstanding personality he did with us initially, because he had been wounded and had to be looked after. And he wasn't passed from soldier to soldier the way the other dogs were. He became closely attached to one of my patrol commanders, Sergeant Fielding. In fact, he really became Fielding's dog.

'As I understand it, Rat shared a room with Sergeant Fielding and Sergeant Regan. Their room, incidentally, was right next to the Officers' Mess and the Ops Room. So there was this dog either resting in the Ops Room or sleeping in Fielding's room. When Fielding was out on patrol, Rat, I believe, slept on his bed. He did a lot of sleeping at this time, I remember. Then Fielding began to take him out on patrol, initially into the village.'

As Tim Fielding recalls the matter, the dog, now perky

and lively again, began by attaching himself closely to him.

'He followed me everywhere I went,' he says. As a Welsh Guardsman who later knew Rat well described his association, '*You* didn't choose Rat as a friend—*he* chose you.'

'And of course, I quickly became very fond of him.' At this stage, Rat was still greatly attracted by Sarrycans; that is, his greatest pleasure in life, after sleep, food and being patted on the head, was simply to ride in an armoured car.

One day, Sergeant Fielding was due to go on helicopter patrol. Helicopters by now were proving important weapons in patrolling the straggling almost-300-mile-long border between Northern Ireland and the Republic, across which small units of the IRA were constantly slipping to attack the army or firebomb property and then retreat south again. Fielding snatched up the animal, stuffed Rat's legs and most of his body down his jacket, leaving Rat's head to emerge like a baby kangaroo from its mother's pouch, and took the dog up for what was possibly his first ride in a helicopter. Some animals might have been frightened, but Rat took to the air like Biggles. He delighted in the experience, and from then on, it became difficult to keep him out of helicopters.

Although he never allowed Fielding to go out on patrol without obediently trotting at his heels or running smartly ahead 'to clear the way', such was his love of army life that he would go out with almost any patrol.

As soon as one patrol came in, Rat would wait expectantly, and then, if he were not yet ready to doze or to eat, would immediately tag along with the next. In fact, although no one could have foreseen it then, Rat had embarked on a self-imposed 'schedule of duties' which was, ultimately, to exhaust him.

'He patrolled with me, or anybody he wanted to go out with,' says Major Woodrow. 'But I can remember lots of times seeing the patrol waiting outside the base to be picked up, and the dog would be sitting there, too, waiting to go with them. Fielding or somebody would just reach down and stuff him inside their jacket. Everybody knew who he was.'

Sergeant Fielding was certain that the sight of Rat, perky, self-confident, eager, leading a patrol as it moved around the town or out into the lush countryside, with its thick hedges, tall grass and sudden little streams, was a great morale-booster for the men. There was something reassuring about the little figure, half-strutting, half-waddling briskly and happily ahead, as though all were right with the world, and death and violence merely a bad dream.

What particularly endeared Rat to Sergeant Fielding (and in due course to the other men in the Company with whom he patrolled) was his intelligence. When a patrol stopped, Rat immediately dropped to his belly on the ground and crouched there, silent and expectant, until the order came to move off. Out in the country, in those dangerous fields where a booby trap might be hidden anywhere, Rat was constantly alert for the patrol commander's orders or the 'brick's' dispositions. If members of a unit stopped to eat 'in the defence position', Rat would mooch quietly over to the gunners who were 'on stag' and lie down alongside them like a sentry.

'I only tried to teach him one thing,' says Sergeant

Fielding. 'Not to bark on patrols—but he still continued to do so.'

The inability to control his barking never proved a handicap. In the event, indeed, almost as though he had attended a personal counter-terrorist course, Rat reserved any signal he chose to make—which included a wide range, from pricked ears and raised tail, through a soft growl to an out-and-out bark—for those occasions when he deemed it necessary to warn the patrol there were strangers ahead or approaching.

In effect, his presence tended to protect patrols rather than to give away their positions, but throughout his service with the army, commanders were careful not to put his brains and intelligence under too strenuous a test. Where it was necessary for a patrol to move with the utmost stealth, Rat generally found himself, to everybody's regret, confined to quarters.

Not that such a restriction was easy to impose or that most patrols wanted to impose it. Although Rat continued to be 'Tim Fielding's dog' and to sleep and eat on his bunk, the lure of action and the excitement of the patrol were frequently too much for his loyalty to Sergeant Fielding. This held particularly good for those periods when Fielding was on guard duties at the base and not leading a patrol. On such occasions, Rat waddled forth to 'show the way' to any patrol which went out.

Sergeant Knight recalls one special night patrol when both Rat and Fleabus turned up unexpectedly and, at first, seemed to him to pose a threat to the operation. Although, around the camp, Rat and Fleabus were inseparable, Fleabus himself was rarely seen out with a patrol.

Indeed, although the pre-eminence that Rat achieved with the men and the relative lack of recognition accorded to Fleabus (and other camp dogs, including one named 'Nutter') depended largely, in the first instance, on Rat's personality and appeal, it was also due to two other factors which worked in his favour, and against Fleabus in particular.

First, Fleabus invariably chose to hang about camp and rarely if ever to accompany a patrol. He thus failed to share the full dangers of operations with the troops as did Rat. Secondly, there was the question of size; Rat, fortunately, was small. Fleabus was a black Labrador cross-breed that loomed large and kept getting in everybody's way inside the base's cramped quarters.

Sergeant Knight and his patrol were due for a Night Patrol and Op in a remote farmhouse which they had been ordered to occupy till daylight. They left camp at approximately 2000 hours, moving in pitch dark. They had gone only a short distance when they heard movement to the rear. At once, the entire patrol dropped on to their stomachs and, with weapons poised for action, stiffened into silence, listening. The rustling sounds grew louder and dramatic action seemed imminent. And then, suddenly, there in their midst were Rat and Fleabus!

The presence of the dogs gave Sergeant Knight several anxious moments. There was the obvious danger that they might bark and give away the patrol's position. He tried to shoo them away, but Rat merely wagged his tail and pointed his nose up at him as if expecting to be patted on the head. Knight, however, was anything but friendly; men's lives were at risk, and he could not take chances. Despairingly, he decided to cancel the patrol. But just as he was about to order the patrol back he saw Rat run forward and start sniffing vigorously all over the ground that lay ahead.

'It at once occurred to me that if anybody had been to my front, waiting to ambush my patrol, Rat and the other dog would have reacted by barking. So I decided to proceed to my target.'

As Knight gave the order to move forward, and the patrol edged its way carefully and cautiously towards the farmhouse, the dogs constantly kept several yards ahead, casting a wide net.

'At each stage, the dogs would come back to the patrol. Then they would go forward again, sniffing, and then we would proceed. The reason why I carried on was because I felt that the dogs were proving to be more of a help than a hindrance. We finally reached the target area safely, and once we were stationary, the dogs left without any bother at all, which surprised my section and me. Next morning, when we got back to camp, there were the two of them, waiting for us, right as rain, and Rat as perky as ever.'

As days lengthened into weeks and weeks into months, Rat in particular (and the Grenadier Guards insist that he was always 'Rat' to them and not 'Rats') became a focal point for the soldiers' pent-up feelings of warmth and affection and kindness. Aside altogether from that natural affinity between dog and man, these young soldiers had few ways of expressing these natural feelings.

Crossmaglen was an exceedingly dangerous town; too many soldiers had already died there. Apart from the danger, Crossmaglen was not all that different from many small towns in Britain, and, indeed, because it had not been blighted by industrial wastes, might even have

43

appeared quite bearable under normal circumstances. It could have been just another place where soldiers, when off duty, could have wandered into the local pubs, mingled sociably with local inhabitants, or attended local dances and taken out local girls. None of these harmless activities, however was possible.

Had these young men been set down in some remote desert fortress, then the sense of deprivation and isolation might not have been so great. But the sight of what outwardly appeared to be a normal little town, inhabited by a presumably normal people—housewives, public-house landlords, shopkeepers, motorists, schoolchildren, even a priest or two—busy going about their normal duties, and almost *totally ignoring them*, proved disturbing to British troops. Efforts at normal intercourse were stiffly repulsed by the locals. Soldiers were not welcome, and only children, who would call out to Rat by name—after the soldiers had told it to them—or pat him on the head, showed any signs of friendliness.

'The reason I found the local people were not very friendly to us was because they were frightened,' says Sergeant Fielding. 'But they were very polite, and even friendly when they were on their own—when nobody could see them. The only people who were always hostile to us were the hard-core Republicans.'

In fact, as in many other Catholic areas of Northern Ireland, it was dangerous to show friendliness to the 'occupiers'; this could be taken as a betrayal of the Old Cause, which could bring its own reprisals. Generally, the locals would answer questions when asked, and never put themselves into a position where the army could find cause to arrest or harass them. But their attitude remained stoic and, in general, unbending. Natural Irish warmth and gregariousness only exhibited itself on rare occasions when it was thought that other hostile eyes could not see them. Collaboration with the British Army at any level whatever invited reprisals from the IRA.

As Rat, in particular, became more and more important to the soldiers—'he became important to us because he was *one* of us,' explains Sergeant Fielding—worries about his whereabouts often became mingled with ordinary regard for his well-being.

'I don't think there were ever any signs of hostility shown towards Rat while we were there,' says Major Woodrow. 'I think you've got to understand the general reaction of the locals to dogs. To them, unlike city folk— and I'm not suggesting that this makes them more backward than city people, just different—dogs in general were work animals. The locals, I think, did not generally see dogs as pets. So it would possibly never have occurred to them to try and understand what Rat had come to mean to the Grenadiers. So I don't think the locals really paid any attention to him—at least not while we were there.

'The trouble was that you could never be sure if the Opposition had decided to pick off Rat or nab him or do something horrible to him. I remember while we were serving in Belfast some years before, the Opposition got hold of one of our pets. Often they just strung army pets up but, this time, they skinned the animal. Now, that wasn't a nice thought, and knowing that there were twisted people about, I sometimes worried when Rat didn't appear for a while. You see, one saw him all the time and I can remember on one occasion, anxiously demanding to know, "Where the hell is he?" and feeling a little degree of worry. After all, he was part of the Company, part of our life. And the effect on the men's feelings had to be considered if somebody tossed him over the wire one night.'

Sergeant Fielding explains, 'We'd have all been very angry, very angry indeed, if anything had happened to him.'

As it was, Rat, despite the dangers, was busy enjoying the life of Reilly. He would paddle into the Ops Room and curl up there for a while, listening to all the exciting telephone calls and other activity. Then he discovered even more delights in the Officers' Mess, particularly as winter set in, dark, cold, wet and generally miserable.

First, there was a cosy gas fire before which to warm himself. Then a TV set. Then, also, a fridge.

'That fridge,' recalls Major Woodrow, 'had some very expensive food in it, particularly coming up to Christmas. I mean, we weren't getting any leave that Christmas, so the fridge had lots of stuff from England, food which had been sent out for the officers, not for him—but in the end, he managed to get his share of it. Perhaps more than his share.'

In fact Rat's standard of living at this period makes a total mockery of the phrase 'a dog's life'. In itself the gas fire was a tremendous luxury—and a tremendous magnet. He even staked out a claim to his own special chair in the Officers' Mess.

'He used to sit there, in this chair, looking absolutely *revolting*,' says Major Woodrow. 'Oh, by this time, of course, he had gained the affections of us all—but I still thought him revolting.'

The trouble was, of course, that even Rat, despite all his

activities and exercise, could not properly assimilate the sheer tonnage and variety of food then being proffered him. It was common enough for the cooks to slip him an extra steak or string of sausages. Then Tim Fielding or one of the other Grenadiers would make sure that he received his proper rations. Then he would wander into the Officer's Mess and perhaps somebody would open a Fortnum's hamper and offer him a titbit.

'I think you have got to accept that if you have a dog in an army base, a lot of soldiers will give him things to eat,' says Major Woodrow. 'The worst thing is that this is food a dog would not normally eat. So they'd stuff him with chocolate and then somebody else would follow that up with chips. So the poor dog eventually gave in and was sick. I don't think it was a matter of him being overfed so much as being fed the wrong things. You know, we had no dog biscuits or anything like that for him. So when you ask me what my memories of Rat are, I have this recollection of him being sick in the Mess or waking up in the morning and finding he had been sick. I think there was one occasion when he was sick in the middle of the night. To be absolutely fair to the little fellow, he wasn't sick all that often. And you couldn't say it was his fault.

'So we did our best for him. And I had him looked at by an army vet. I believe we sent him up to Bessbrook, to Battalion HQ, once or twice to have him checked.'

As Company Commander, Major Woodrow took the view that Rat was an asset on most patrols.

'There is no question that where you might have had bombs that are triggered by weight or by wire or something like that, Rat was performing a really useful job. He would trigger them, if that sort of trap were there. On the whole, though, he just went out with the patrols, bit the odd Irishman and came back. He was not a noisy dog in any way. And certainly anything but ferocious—so far as humans were concerned. I think you've got to realise the extraordinarily isolated position we were all in to realise why he gained such a hold on our affections. When you're away from home for maybe five months at a time, you tend to look after and worry about the things that are around you. In this case, it was a dog—just that. Just a human reaction. And after all, why should we have thrown him out? Why shouldn't we have made a fuss of him? He was a perfectly amiable little chap who wandered around the base causing virtually no trouble at all.'

In fact, looked at in another way, Rat undoubtedly did his best to earn the love and affection that was lavished on him. Not only did he respond faithfully to the men, returning their care and regard with at least an equal tenderness; not only did he prove, as one soldier put it, 'that there was something Irish that wasn't hostile to us', which enabled the men to feel less isolated and cut off; but in the event, he was to prove his value at a moment when, under threat, a 'brick' could easily have made an error and perhaps opened fire on another patrol.

In more ways than one, then, Rat was to prove himself a true soldiers' friend.

FOUR

For some time after Kevin Kinton had been wounded, he felt both bitter and angry.

His father had approved when he had originally told him he was joining the army, and although his mother also believed that this would be a good thing, both training him and teaching him discipline which he could put to good use later, he had noticed how worried she had appeared when he told her that he was being sent to Ireland, although she had tried to hide her feelings.

His father, too, might have been concerned but he did not show it; he admired his son and he felt proud of him.

When Kevin Kinton went back on patrol again he moved more warily than on his arrival in Crossmaglen. He was more watchful and justifiably suspicious of everyone he saw. It hardly helped that the locals remained hostile; after all, what had he done to *them*? He was there in an attempt to keep the peace, not to provoke it.

Later, fortunately, they would appear to be more friendly, but then they also felt resentful at the memory of ways in which they considered that previous regiments had 'harassed' them. Now when Kinton took up a defensive position in a doorway, and a local woman walked past him, if he tried to speak to her, simply to wish her 'good morning', she might spit on him.

If under orders he asked her any questions about the

movements of any cars or people in the town, she would just stare coldly ahead, walking on and completely ignoring him. The soldiers felt that in Crossmaglen at least they could be certain of one thing only; if a local resident spoke to them at all it was to abuse them.

And yet, as the weeks merged into a month or more, an important change gradually began to take place. The Grenadiers with their splendid discipline and bearing, with their strict attention to protocol and the detached way in which they ignored insults and abuse alike, slowly began to establish better relations with the people of Crossmaglen.

These were never to become in any way warm, but at least people began to wish them 'good morning', or would pass some such remark to them as, 'It's a cold day, isn't it?' They still kept a careful distance, of course, never allowing relations to become too close.

The Grenadiers tried their best to break down these barriers of resentment, partly in the hope that by so doing they would win an important battle in the war for minds and hearts, and partly because it was sometimes necessary to check on the movements of certain characters, either locals or visitors.

In an effort to keep track of potential terrorists, it was essential to check public-houses and the shops, and to ask people where they were going so that the army knew where everybody lived, and could put a name and a face to people in every house, or involved with each shop or pub in the town. A strange face, an unknown name, could always arouse suspicion.

The IRA, of course, knew this, which was why local people, in general, still refused to talk, and turned away rather than become involved.

At Christmas the Company set up a Christmas tree in the base and a few decorations and every soldier had two extra cans of beer with his Christmas dinner, but it had been a depressing experience all the same, tramping the desolate streets, seeing the inhabitants 'getting the booze in' and putting up decorations and generally developing a festive mood.

New Year's Eve was cold and raining hard as it had been raining for three days. But as Corporal Kinton led his patrol past a house, he heard the door open and a man's voice call out, 'Why don't you come in? Do you want a drink?'

This was 'the first time anything like that had happened to me in Crossmaglen,' says Kinton, who replied, 'I can't come in. I've got the rest of the "brick" here.'

The man answered, 'You're soaking wet. Bring the boys in round the back.'

So the 'brick' went round to the rear of the house, through the little garden, and sat down in front of the kitchen fire, where the man served each of them with a glass of rum and a share of a pork pie.

'I want to make it plain,' says Sergeant Kinton now, 'that I never felt resentment against the local population in general. I took the view that, so far as most of them were concerned, they had nothing to do with the trouble. They had no control over what was happening—it was the IRA. And I didn't know where the IRA man who blew me up came from. He might have lived in the town. He might have lived out in the country. He might have been from somewhere else altogether. So I was never against the people there.

'For a while, I attempted to find out who had been responsible, trying my own little bit of detective work. But I never did find out. So one was left feeling sometimes that here were people who might say "good morning" to you one moment—and then attempt to kill you the next—which was an extraordinary feeling.

'I think they soon realised that we weren't as "awkward", from their point of view, as some of the earlier regiments who had been stationed there had been, for they hadn't, perhaps, been too gentle with them when the troubles were at their height. Towards the end of our tour, even the men in the town began to co-operate with us. One of our regular jobs was stopping cars at VCPs and checking boots and bonnets in case anyone was attempting to smuggle through arms or ammunition. At first, they'd slam the door angrily and shout at you. Near the end, they would be quite affable and say, "Sure, look inside." '

Rat, for his part, loved 'working' on VCPs.

'It was as if he were trying to be a soldier himself,' recalls Kinton. 'If you were going to stop a car as part of a checkpoint job, Rat would run ahead and start biting at the tyres and wheels as the car braked, as though personally trying to make it stop. He seemed to believe he was helping to control the car, just like a soldier.'

Kevin Kinton had his bunk in the big eighteen-man dormitory, and although by general consent Rat had been allocated a bunk of his own, 'he preferred to sleep on somebody else's. He'd even try to sneak in under the bed covers if you let him.' Every time a patrol went out, Kinton or one of the other brick commanders would ask Rat, 'Are you coming for walkies?' And if Rat were up to it, he would immediately go along.

'At home I'd had a dog of my own, a Labrador called Scamp, so I suppose that, like most of the other men, I missed the company of my dog. But whether you owned a dog yourself or not, it wouldn't have made very much difference. We were all lonely out there, and the dog was something, indeed the *only* thing, we could give affection to. And the little dog responded. He responded to us like a soldier, like one of the boys.

'The other dogs around the camp were lazy things, really, and I suppose they didn't earn or deserve the attention Rat received. He was more energetic. He was perky and he was cuter. Even though Rat and Fleabus were together in the camp all the time, Fleabus never caught our imaginations in the same way.

'You'd see the two dogs lying on a bed together, heads nestling together. But Rat was in charge. In fact, he behaved like a bodyguard to this other dog, always doing things for him, looking after him—he was very intelligent.

'We played with Rat a lot, I remember. He had a sock he had pinched off one of the blokes, and he used to go and hide it. If you found it and went to hide it somewhere for him, he'd perk up immediately and go around looking for his sock. Then we had an old ball which we tossed around, and which he chased.

'The pity was that he was often sick. He was always being fed in the kitchens—somebody would pinch a steak and give it to him—chocolate, anything. But it was marvellous to see him whenever we left the camp. A bunch of dogs outside would be standing, waiting, and they'd maybe start barking at us and Rat, who was a real leader and obviously jealous of his position of authority, would

53

rush at these dogs and chase them off. You could say that he was acting like a sort of bodyguard to us.'

In a sense, it could be argued that Rat sometimes added to the anxieties of a patrol.

'Yes. We would get worried about him sometimes on patrol—but that was better than worrying about yourself too much, wasn't it? I mean, we were always worried that he would get run over, the way he chased after cars, biting and snarling at the wheels or tyres. He didn't come out much at night with us, but if he did, then he stuck very close to us. I remember one night walking around the town, and it was very cold and wet, and so we went into the Sarrycan for a cup of tea.

'Rat jumped right in after us and sat on our laps—just to keep warm. He always stuck by us. If we took up a position in a doorway, squatting down and trying to keep out of the wind, he would come and stand right by us, stuck up against us, trying to keep the wind off himself, I suppose. I must say he never barked, never gave away our position. In fact, he was useful because he kept all the other dogs of the town away.'

The attitude of the children in Crossmaglen towards Rat was ambivalent. Sometimes they would call out in a friendly way to the little fellow or even pat him on the head. Then it would seem that somebody reminded them that Rat was an army dog and, for this reason, an enemy, and so one of the children might try to kick him. In that case, Rat would run away and take up a defensive position between a guardsman's feet.

'But no one *really* ever tried to take it out on him,' says Sergeant Kinton.

Indeed he recalls one moment when children, soldiers

and dog had a marvellous time together after a heavy snowfall.

'The kids were standing about the street corners, pitching snowballs at each other. So a friendly little snowball fight began between them and our patrol. It proved to be quite amusing, for there was Rat, in between the two sides, snapping and biting at the snowballs as they were tossed through the air. But I noticed one thing—he only snapped and bit at the snowballs the kids threw at us! He was still trying to protect us. He was always protective.'

Back in the camp, Rat continued to prove a tremendous solace. He would jump up on laps, hoping for his head to be patted or caressed. He would roll over on his back so that his tummy could be tickled.

'If he hadn't been out on patrol with us, he was always waiting at the gate to welcome us when we returned. He would make a little noise first, then jump up and down and wag his tail. I'd pat him down, and he'd follow us in when we went to eat.

'He loved to hog the gas fires in the camp. He would take all the heat away, so you'd have to prod him away with your boot, or slide him gently across the floor. But before you knew it, he would have crawled right back again. He would somehow go around the back of where you were sitting and sneak back an inch or so at a time.

'When he was tired, he lay on somebody's bed. If you were resting yourself, he would sometimes come and lie on the bed with you. He would curl up in a corner near your feet. Inevitably, he would start sprawling across your legs, and eventually he'd get kicked off. He could be a little irritating at times, of course. But then everybody irritates somebody sometimes, don't they? When you were trying

55

to get some sleep, for example, Rat would come and scratch against your face—or you'd find him trying to get inside the bed covers with you. So you'd have to shout, "Get away!" and push him off. He wanted to be where the warmth was—where you were lying.'

The great moments of Rat's life, however, continued to be helicopter rides.

'He was always trying to climb into helicopters. In fact, he would always be the first one in—and the first out. As soon as a helicopter started up, there was Rat climbing on to the first step—and then jumping and scrambling the rest of the way in. When the aircraft was hovering down for a landing, he would often jump out from a really considerable height—but somehow he never hurt himself.

'He couldn't always get *into* a helicopter all that easily, particularly if you had landed in a field somewhere, and the helicopter was ready to take off again and almost in the air. Then you'd simply grab him and carry him in. On patrols in the helicopter we took good care he couldn't jump out. Sometimes we would put him in a bergen (a pack) with his head sticking out and his body tied so that he couldn't leap out. We'd put him down on the floor, in the bergen, near the door.

'Some dogs would have gone wild at this treatment, but Rat knew what was going on and obviously enjoyed it. At other times, somebody kept hold of him in their lap. As soon as the helicopter began coming down to land, he was all alert and seemed to know exactly what was happening. Then, before you could touch down, he was out of your lap and streaking for the door—and taking a great leap out into space in an absolutely breathtaking way.'

Rat had been scruffy and fairly dirty when the Grenadiers first took him over.

'One Marine had been determined to take him back to England, but he had been ordered not to—so the Marines passed him on to us, saying, "Well, he's made things a bit more bearable around here, so we're passing him on to you, and we hope he'll make things a bit more bearable for you," ' says Sergeant Kinton. Now Rat was smartened and spruced up in Guards fashion.

'If he ever had fleas, the medics soon made sure he was as clean as possible. He was certainly washed quite a few times, because there was so much mud around the camp that everybody got a bit dirty. We'd just put him in the showers and wash him there. No, I can't say he loved that. In fact, I'm told that sometimes he would run away to try and avoid a wash, and you'd have to chase him and grab hold of him. But I believe nearly all dogs are the same, aren't they?'

So the tour continued. The weather remained mostly cold, and if it was not particularly cold, it became very wet instead. Mentally, there was constant strain. All the time, everyone had to be alert. And then there was the problem of sleep; men were allowed only four hours' sleep at a time. Commanders made sure that everyone had eight hours' sleep in every twenty-four but these rest periods were broken up, so that the routine became a four-hour sleep followed by a spell of duty, then back again for another four hours, before going out on patrol again. Everybody grew used to this spartan routine, but at the start of the tour it proved to be wearing.

In between times most off-duty periods were spent enjoying a quiet snooze or writing letters home. Sergeant

Kinton wrote mostly to his mother—'And she took a great interest in Rat, so I usually mentioned him.' Tim Fielding for his part kept his West German fiancée, Silvia Wanger, up to date with the little dog's doings.

There were darts or cards or even chess games, but most spare time was occupied writing home to mothers or to wives or girl-friends, or simply watching TV. If Rat were around, a soldier might play about with him.

'He seemed to be always trying to act like one of us humans,' says Sergeant Kinton. 'He wanted to be treated as just another soldier. If we started to play a game together, he immediately mucked in with us. I remember once, when a few of us began to kick an old can round the briefing room, we'd only given it a kick or two when Rat got hold of it in his mouth and scampered off. Then he would drop it. But as soon as one of us kicked it, he was off after it again.'

For most of the Grenadiers, the tour in Crossmaglen was one that left them with mixed memories and feelings. None has any hesitation in describing the experience as basically 'frightening' but one that, in the words of one of them, 'I wouldn't have missed for anything'.

Tim Fielding says, 'You had to put all your soldiering experience to the test. I admit I felt frightened on nearly every patrol, because on an earlier tour I had seen three men get killed in Crossmaglen. But it was a tour I wouldn't have missed. It demanded politeness and understanding. It also demanded courage, and it taught you how to overcome your fears.'

Kevin Kinton says: 'I appreciated the experience , and if I had to serve in Ireland again. I'd prefer to go to Crossmaglen than anywhere else. After all, you saw action there. It's a dangerous place all right, but I was a soldier, after all. It was a bit like taking up a dare. The point is that you knew it was a bad place, and you had to accept the challenge—to try and tame this trouble, to achieve law and order there again, which is a worthwhile achievement. And there was also the challenge to your own courage. I feel pleased that I learned to conquer any fears I had.'

Soldiering in this small South Armagh town was not the harrowing experience for the Grenadiers that some had anticipated. They had gone there expecting the worst, and for most of them, there was an odd, yet not unwelcome, excitement about it all.

'Some tours can be boring,' says one of them now. 'But in Crossmaglen you knew that something could happen— just like that! It was real soldiering. And that's why we had joined the army, after all.'

The sheer deceptiveness of the atmosphere was dangerous, of course. Normality can be an insidious thing, picking away at a man's alertness, seducing him into a feeling that everything is as safe and ordinary as it appears on the surface.

Kevin Kinton, for instance, was to escape death narrowly again on two occasions. He had been on duty at a VCP with his 'brick' three days before Christmas and had just been relieved when the second incident occurred. He had had his own 'brick' carefully positioned on the edge of the town, taking advantage of any cover available and then the relieving 'brick' commander, who knew exactly where Kinton was, and where he had his men stationed, signalled, 'I'm coming towards you.'

Kinton had a Sarrycan covering the road for protection and now, as he prepared to go off duty, he called it up to take himself and his 'brick' back to camp.

'I was always scared of being blown up again or being ambushed, you see,' says Sergeant Kinton. 'So I suppose I was more keyed up than most "brick" commanders and I used to shout at the lads to make sure that they didn't get lackadaisical or anything like that, and make sure they took proper cover, either kneeling down or lying down or standing in a doorway; anything but leaving themselves defenceless in the open.'

As the Sarrycan juddered down the road, he noticed that the new 'brick' had taken up different positions to those occupied by his own men. The Sarrycan had just taken them round the corner when Kinton heard the sound of gunfire.

During the time he had been checking at the VCP, in fact, Kinton had noticed an old van parked at the side of the road about three or four hundred metres away. It appeared to have been abandoned, and during the time he had kept it under observation, there had been no sign of life near it. The new patrol was just standing at the side of the road when three men inside the van opened up on them with machine guns.

'There was heavy firing, lasting altogether for about thirty seconds. One, two, three, they opened fire—and three Guardsmen got hit right away. Only the "brick" commander escaped. He was standing behind a wall and so they couldn't hit him. He fired off his rounds at the van as it pulled away but the terrorists seemed to have protected themselves with a wall of breeze blocks inside the vehicle.

'As it drove off, the commander dashed out into the road, grabbed up a machine gun which had been dropped

Rats on parade.

Above: Rats and helicopter party about to board.

Opposite top: Waiting for take-off.
Opposite foot: First out.

Above: On patrol.

Opposite: On the lookout, Crossmaglen.

Above: Rats receiving the congratulations of Mrs Scott-Ordish of "Pro-Dogs" after winning the 1979 Gold Medal Award.

Opposite: In the cockpit.

Rats with medal and handler, Corporal Lewis, after the Pro-Dog
Award ceremony.

by one of the dead "brick" and blazed away after them. Then he chased after them—but they got away. It was a terrible ambush, with three men dead. Two died instantly and the third in a helicopter on his way to hospital.'

In the general mêlée, it appears, Rat, who had been scurrying about somewhere, escaped without a mark.

The brave little 'soldier' was not so fortunate at the next incident, about a month after Christmas, when Sergeant Kinton was leading his 'brick' around the town.

'I was very, very careful by now,' he says, 'particularly about parked cars, which I always gave a wide berth. If I saw a parked car, I would deliberately take to the middle of the road. I knew, of course, that this might leave me open to a sniper—but, to be honest, I'd sooner be sniped at with a rifle than blown up by a bomb. Besides, you always stand the chance of being missed by a sniper.

'I instructed my "brick" to walk down the middle of the road as we had to pass a purple-coloured parked car. When we had passed the spot where I had been blown up previously, and were about fifty metres or so nearer the camp, I saw another patrol coming out and approaching us.

'As we passed this patrol, I noticed that they were what we call "working the pavements". That is, two of the "brick" were walking on one pavement and two on the opposite side. We had just walked through the camp gates when we heard the explosion from what proved to be another radio-controlled petrol bomb, which had been placed in the purple-coloured car.

'The IRA had mixed a couple of gallons of petrol with explosives and placed them in the car boot and so the car exploded like a big firebomb. One of our men caught the full blast and was set on fire, and began running round the street like a human torch. Fortunately, the other members of his "brick" managed to put the flames out. He was very badly burned however, and spent a long time in hospital. After such a narrow escape, I can tell you, I had this feeling that the IRA or somebody was out to get me personally. You can't help thinking this way.'

Another casualty was Rat, who lost much of his tail in this incident. IRA firebombs are often made of a cunning mixture of explosives, using petrol and a gooey ball of washing-powder flakes. So when a firebomb explodes, flakes shoot up in a spray of flame. They spread out in the air and stick fast to any objects on which they land. Some of these flakes, it appears, landed on Rat's tail. They burned the poor dog badly, and left him with only a three-inch stump of tail to wag.

A major problem for the security forces—on both sides of the border—was the apparent ease with which IRA bombers could carry out an attack in Northern Ireland and then slip south to safety. This was, in effect, like a reprise of an old Hollywood film where the wanted men escape the law's clutches by crossing the State line, for once the terrorists were in the Republic, the army had to break off pursuit.

Helicopters introduced a new element into this un-satisfactory situation. A helicopter could overfly in a matter of minutes an area which might take foot patrols hours or even days to search. As a result, Major Woodrow tried to make an aerial reconnaissance at least once every day above that sensitive border which was little more than a stone's throw from the Crossmaglen camp.

One day, late in January 1979, the Major was leading a helicopter patrol in a broad sweep above the border, while, on the ground, Sergeant Fielding was leading a foot patrol over the same area.

As Woodrow swept over the emerald-dark, sodden countryside, he saw two vehicles. About 20 men were travelling in a car and an open truck which appeared to have a mortar baseplate fitted in the back. He decided to land immediately and check these vehicles. Major Woodrow radioed for reinforcements. As the helicopter came in to land, the suspects opened fire, and a fierce gun-battle began.

A mile or so away, Sergeant Fielding heard the radio call and instantly commandeered two passing cars, packed his patrol members in them and raced to the spot—accompanied by the indefatigable and omnipresent Rat with teeth bared.

The terrorists, whose tactics were always to avoid open combat whenever possible, reversed their vehicles and raced south over the border.

The British army never under-rated their adversary, and in the opinion of most soldiers who have served in South Armagh, the IRA were arguably the most dangerous and effective guerrilla organisation in the world, capable of testing the army's ability to contain this type of 'guerrilla warfare' to the limit. As Sergeant Kinton says, 'It was real soldiering—and every bit as dangerous for the individual soldier as a world war.'

The IRA were a devious and ingenious enemy—as Major Woodrow discovered when, ten days later, once more sweeping along above the border, he again spotted two vehicles—this time a van and another lorry, also seemingly equipped to act as a mobile base for a mortar attack.

'Of course, it was a trap,' says Major Woodrow now. 'A set-up. We were just coming in to have a look, when they opened fire on us—very heavily indeed.

'They hit us with a heavy calibre 7.62, probably an M60, and a couple of Bren guns. The helicopter was hit about nine times and I personally was hit three times. I took a crease and two proper shots. The pilot was hurt quite badly, with shrapnel in his face, and a young officer riding in the back was also badly wounded.

'We couldn't have continued anyway, for they had hit the rotor blade, with the result that the aircraft became very unstable. They were firing tracers at us, and one shot set the machine on fire, although we managed to put this out fairly quickly.

'With the pilot in a state of shock, we were lucky, I suppose, to make it back to base. And, that, so far as I was concerned, was the end of my time in Crossmaglen. I was taken to hospital in Belfast, where I stayed until it was time for the Battalion to return to England. I was flown back with intravenous drips, and all that sort of thing. I never saw Rat again—and I do insist that he was *Rat* to us—and, to be quite honest, I had a lot of other things to think about.

'On reflection, he did a lot for our morale. He was cheerful, very happy and never really a nuisance, and it was always pleasant to have a little animal to give you a warm welcome when you came back off patrol.'

Kevin Kinton, Michael Knight and, of course, Tim Fielding were all sorry to say good-bye to Rat as the Grenadiers pulled out and handed over to the 1st Battalion, The Queen's Lancashire Regiment.

Sergeant Knight remembered nights he had spent in the Ops Room, the only man on duty, with Rat as his sole companion.

Keith Regan, who won the BEM for his work in Crossmaglen and who had possibly saved the little dog's life after he had been blown up, recalled moments when Rat had become mixed up with his legs when he was trying to work the film projector for the Company.

Kevin Kinton's memories were, of course, much grimmer, but he too had known and valued the friendship of the 'little dog-soldier'.

Rat, naturally, was there to see them all leave. One by one, they patted his head before they climbed aboard the chopper. Sergeant Fielding was easily the saddest person in the party. At one stage, indeed, he had felt so gloomy about parting with the dog he planned to take him back to England. But knowing that the Battalion was shortly due to go to Germany, he realised that he would have to let him stay.

'I'll never forget the day we left, though,' he says. 'As we went to get on the helicopter, Rat ran with us to try and climb aboard. I had to pick him up firmly, tuck him under my arm and carry him back to the man who was taking over from me. As the helicopter was taking off, I sat looking down at him through the door and it almost broke my heart. There he was whining and struggling, fighting to come aboard with us. I have no doubt, no doubt at all, but that he knew we were leaving him, and that he might never see any of us again. All I can say is that he had been a blessing to all of us while we were there. So far as any dog could, he had made us happy . . .'

FIVE

It may have been that Rat was grieving; or it may have been that his house manners had improved. Anyway, with The Queen's Lancashire Regiment now occupying the base, Rats (as they called him) forsook his old habit of lying *on* bunks and, instead, opted to sleep *under* them.

Unlike his association with the Grenadier Guards, he was slow to make a special friend although, in the end, he did make a pal of Corporal Ainsworth. As with the regiments with whom he had served earlier, all soldiers, basically, were his chums. For a while, therefore, he did not favour anybody specially, but slept under different bunks as the fancy took him.

One night, after an exhausting four-hour patrol, Rats crept under the bunk of Corporal Hayward and here he snoozed gently until Hayward woke up to go out on patrol. As the corporal reached down for his flak jacket, his searching fingers found Rats' tail instead, and, on an impulse, he tweaked it.

The main point about Rats, all in every regiment are agreed, is that there could not be a more loving, faithful or protective dog. Yet there are limits, even for such a dog—and Corporal Hayward had overstepped them. To the delight of the entire section, Rats' head snapped round and he bit the offending hand. As Hayward's protest reached the ceiling, the entire dormitory roared with laughter.

On the whole, however, Rats remained as he had always been: ready to defend his comrades, to do his duty and, in particular, to protect his patrol. On one patrol, the section suddenly found itself face to face with a big Pyrenean dog which apparently had Republican political leanings, and decided that a bite or two out of a British army leg might do wonders for this cause.

As the section stood by to defend itself, Rats leaped bravely to the front and took up an aggressive position between the Pyrenean and his patrol leader. For a second or two, as the event has been described, it was a scene reminiscent of 'David and Goliath'. If the Pyrenean had possessed any sense, of course, he would at this juncture have retreated. Instead, he essayed an attack. Rats naturally stood his ground, and then dived suddenly at the Pyrenean's legs. The big dog had no answer to this ferocious counter-offensive, and within a minute or so had given up the fight, and was running away up the road with Rats in pursuit.

Although, by now, Rats had been creased savagely by bullets, blown up by high-explosives and partially set on fire by a petrol-bomb, and although he appeared to risk his life every time his section manned a checkpoint by his insistence on attacking the wheels of cars, he clearly bore a charmed existence. His courage remained remarkable and his indomitable spirit seemed incapable of being quenched.

Once, while on patrol, Rats stepped on a broken bottle and had to have his leg stitched by Corporal Copperthwaite, the Company medic. The main danger to his well-being, however, was still likely to arise from his habit of attacking all cars or other moving vehicles, as though they were mortal enemies. He would courageously advance to meet them as they approached a VCP, and chase them down the road for twenty or thirty yards after they had gone through, as though to see them properly through the checkpoint and on their way.

One April day, he was chasing a car, darting at its wheels in his normal fashion when the driver—whether on purpose or by accident was never discovered—suddenly lurched to the left without any warning and then accelerated away, leaving an injured Rats in the roadway, yelping with pain. Corporal Ainsworth immediately ran to him and carried him back to base where he reported the 'accident' to the Company Commander.

Rats' left front leg looked bruised, and appeared to be seriously damaged. At once the resources of the British Army were summoned, and the 'casualty' was rushed to Battalion HQ at Bessbrook, and then to the Maze Prison at Long Kesh, where a team of army veterinary surgeons was based. Their job was to care for guard dogs there and they diagnosed that Rats had broken his leg. The senior vet personally set the fractured limb, and within a month Rats was able to return to his duties.

Undeterred, and as full of courage as ever, he was soon back chasing cars or attempting to stop them, literally with his bare teeth. Then he was hurt a second time—this time in collision with a bus. As a result Rats needed stitches in his head. In everybody's opinion, this was a most untypical gesture on the part of Rats, 'who always used his head, all right, but never to stop a bus!'

For some reason, despite his known attachment to

helicopters, RAF pilots appeared reluctant to take him aloft again. Yet his obvious eagerness to be in the air was thoroughly appreciated by the members of the QLR, who managed to circumvent their objections by concealing Rats in their jackets, or hiding him in their bergens, and smuggling him aboard the aircraft.

When the Company used a ground vehicle instead, Rats had a special seat reserved for him.

As a member of the regiment explains, 'There were always three seats reserved. One for the section commander, Paddy Moran; one for the tea urn—and one for Rats.'

Yet this remarkable dog also knew fear—and sometimes showed it. Tigerishly, he would race across a field and scatter a herd of cows—or better still, calves.

'But they sometimes turned on him,' explains Corporal Ainsworth sheepishly, 'and then he would run and take refuge between my legs—which caused me some considerable embarrassment.'

Corporal Joseph O'Neil, 1st Battalion Queen's Own Highlanders, was aged 29 when he arrived in Crossmaglen in August 1979, for his fifth Northern Ireland tour. He had already served for ten years in the army, and although he had been posted to Dungannon, Coalisland and Belfast, he had been spared serious action. He was a Glasgow man, whose father, a semi-skilled slinger, had seen service with the Royal Artillery.

Joseph O'Neil was a Roman Catholic, which made him feel that he was well suited to get on with the local population. At school, his best subjects had been woodwork and

PT. He was also good at sport and had won a medal for football, and another for winning a long jump, and when training at the depot, he had won a tankard for being the best shot in his Company. Ever since, as a boy, he played games of soldiers in the street, he had wanted to join the army.

'I tried to join when I was 17, but my father refused to sign the papers. He insisted that I should learn a trade first. "Then if you don't like the army," he told me, "you've always got your trade." '

So Joseph O'Neil finished his time as a joiner and then he joined the army. He was delighted to serve in Northern Ireland, particularly Crossmaglen, for the same reason as many of his colleagues, 'because otherwise I would have had ten years in the army and seen no real soldiering'.

He had known his wife Christine before joining up and in his words, 'she hadn't been all that pleased about it, really. But when we decided to get married, I told her, "Look, it's me that's going to be the breadwinner, and so it's up to me to do what I think is right."

'She agreed with that. And, anyway, there weren't that many good jobs around in Glasgow, even then. People were always getting laid off and that sort of thing, and I didn't want to be on the dole. I never want to be on the dole—I don't believe in being on it. I've got too much drive and energy to sit down and do nothing. But nothing happens unless you make it happen, I know that. So I decided to try the army, and if I didn't make good, well, I'd come out and try something else.'

He arrived in Crossmaglen just before the birth of their third child. He and Christine already had two sons and desperately wanted a little daughter. The birth was due in

October, and he was hoping he might have leave before Christmas to see the new baby.

He managed to telephone Christine almost every night. There was a telephone box near his home—and if Christine herself couldn't answer it, a neighbour would usually hear it ringing, and go across and knock on her door. There were two small private telephone boxes in the base for the troops to use, so he rarely wrote letters. 'I don't like writing,' he admits.

Early in October, Corporal O'Neil came off patrol around about midnight or one o'clock and put in his usual routine call to his wife. Although the baby was nearly due, there was apparently no change in his wife's condition. He therefore dossed down and went to sleep contentedly.

'About an hour later, I was woken up by the clerk who said, "I've just had a phone call from the hospital." So I jumped up, got through to the hospital, and was told we had a wee girl. I couldn't have been more delighted—because that was what we both wanted. So I went through to the choggie-shop to celebrate Nadine's arrival. This shop is a wee place which sells beer, razor blades, sweets and things like that.

'We were entitled to two cans of beer a day, but as I hadn't had any for a couple of days, I asked for four cans. As I was returning, I ran into the major who asked me, "What are you on, corporal?"

'I told him I was just getting a few beers to celebrate the fact that my wife had had a wee girl.

'"Is this your first?" he asked kindly.

'"No, sir, my third!"

'He looked at me in total astonishment. Celebrating your first was one thing—but your *third*! I don't think he

71

realised how much Christine and I love children.'

When Corporal O'Neil returned to the eighteen-man dormitory he was so excited that he could not keep his good news to himself.

'I kept wakening up my mates to tell them I'd just had a wee lassie, and asking them to have a beer. I kept saying, "I hope she's all right," until one retorted, "Why the hell don't you use the phone and find out?"

'So I got through on the phone and Christine was absolutely chuffed. She asked me how I felt and I told her, "Over the moon." I was given leave a few days later and saw the new bairn, and I was a really happy man when I came back to Crossmaglen.'

Nobody was more pleased to see him back than Rats. Although Rats always, if not immediately, made a special friend of one soldier in every regiment, it is doubtful whether he was ever made a greater fuss of by any of them than by Corporal O'Neil—or was regarded with more affection in return.

'When we first arrived, the corporal who had been looking after him explained that Rats—which I was told was short for Rations—had been handed on from one regiment to the next, and asked me if I would be prepared to take care of him. Believe it or not, Rats wouldn't come to me at first.'

'All you've got to do is feed him a couple of times,' the corporal assured him.

O'Neil, who had been among the advance party of section-leaders and specialists who arrived before the main body of the QOH, in order to facilitate the hand-over, had first encountered Rats on his first patrol. He had come in by helicopter one afternoon, and within three hours was out on patrol 'just to let us see the area'.

Rats 'led' this patrol and, when they returned in the evening, 'Rats walked in ahead of us and made straight for his bunk—that is, the other corporal's bunk—and just lay there while the other corporal was getting washed. After that, the corporal took his eating irons through for a meal and came back with a plate for Rats, who jumped down and started to eat.

'This chap used to play the mouth organ to Rats every evening. I can remember that the dog's favourite tune was that old Petula Clark song, "Sailor". Rats used to sit there and sing! Yes, he would go "yow-yow-yow" sort of thing, accompanying the music. The whole performance kept everybody in stitches and I remember thinking, "This is great. This would take your mind off a lot of worry." After all, as a family man myself, having Rats there was almost like having a kid in the place. That's what Rats was to some of us, certainly to me, a replacement for a child. It made you feel you weren't in Northern Ireland at all, but at home.'

Rats had seemed utterly lost and lonely after his old regiment moved out.

'I was the only person he knew. I found him one evening just sitting beside me and I thought, "Why is he sitting beside me like this? He's never sat beside me before." I thought he was after his supper, so I went through to the cookhouse and brought him back something to eat. But he wouldn't take it at first, and it wasn't until I went out of the room and then returned that I found he had eaten it. He was real fly—much more so than you'd have imagined. You wouldn't think a dog would have much brains, but Rats had brains all right.

73

'Rats, as short for Rations, suited him all right, for he was always eating. He also liked biting at things. He was always at my bootlaces, biting them, when I was on patrol. I went through four pairs in half the time it would take you to think—all thanks to Rats.'

Even if life had been more normal in Crossmaglen; if the troops had been able to mix with locals in pubs, or otherwise pass their spare time more pleasantly, Corporal O'Neil is convinced that he would still have made friends with Rats.

'Once I got to know him, it was great. That first night the other regiment left, he curled up on the other corporal's empty bunk. But then I started to talk to him, "Aren't you going to come and play with me? Aren't you going to come to me?" That sort of thing. I couldn't play the mouth organ, of course, but I could whistle—so I did. Rats was really fond of music, and when I whistled, he would just cock his head and look at me like that dog on the labels of the old HMV records. And then he'd go "yow-yow-yow".

'So that's how we became friends. I'd feed him, rub his tummy, push away his nose and talk to him. A couple of nights later, he obviously decided he was my pal and he jumped on to my bed as I was about to go to sleep. I pushed him off and told him, "Off you go—you've got your own bed."

'But when I woke up, I found him lying beside me. Again I told him, "Get off," and added, "Don't you be starting this with me." But what could you do? He'd decided we were pals and that was that.

'When I started out on patrol that day, he followed me. The next thing I knew, he was savaging my bootlaces. I remember looking down at him and saying, "Oh, so that's it—you're now my friend, are you?" '

Friendship and affection like this brought their own penalties.

'I was always a little worried that something might happen to him. This being Northern Ireland, I always felt that somebody might do something to him. Then for two days he went missing, and I was half out of my mind. He had gone out with another patrol and hadn't come back with them. At first, I didn't think much about it because he was always going out with patrols, and he wouldn't always come back with the patrol he had gone out with. If he met another patrol when he was on the way in, he might go off with them.

'Eventually he did come back—and he'd had his stomach badly ripped open. Somebody who had been on patrol said he had seen Rats with a group of other dogs, and that they had been fighting. They must have given him a good going-over to injure him like that. He might have been bitten—or he might have been attacked. It was hard to tell. But it was a plain cut, not a rip the way it would have been if it had been a dog-bite. It could have been caused by barbed wire—and certainly he was always running into the fields and chasing cows.

'But there's another mystery. He was seen by several patrols while he was supposed to be missing. As soon as they whistled to him, however, Rats turned and ran away. He was seen maybe a hundred and fifty metres away, usually with other dogs, but as soon as the patrol approached, Rats was off, and the other dogs with him. The only explanation we can really think of is that it had to do with his love life. In my view, there was a Mrs Rats out there! That's why we didn't see him for a few days.'

Not that he could be always coaxed to accompany every patrol though.

'He would go out with some and not with others. He *chose* his patrol—just as he chose his friends. They didn't choose him; he chose them. He's a dog who had his own mind, as much as to say: "No, I'm not going with you lot, I'm off on my tod." '

Corporal O'Neil emphasises that 'Rats had character, personality, a mind of his own. He would come and sit and look at you at times as much as to say, "Do you want to play?" He was independent, his own dog, so to speak. If he got a chance, he jumped aboard a helicopter whether anybody was with him or not. He had an awful habit of doing this—and once or twice he jumped aboard without anybody's permission and ended up at Battalion HQ at Bessbrook.

'He was cute. And intelligent. I can give you one example of this that was really amazing. We had been sent out on a covert kind of Op one night, which involved lying out in the countryside, hoping to catch some of the bad boys. You were not really supposed to have a dog along in these circumstances but after we'd started off, I found Rats following us, and although I tried to get rid of him, there was nothing I could do about it. He was usually good however, so I wasn't unduly worried. And, indeed, he sat quiet all night. Next thing I knew he began to bark. We hadn't heard a sound, but we knew somebody must be coming and so we got prepared. This person turned out to be the platoon commander. Luckily he recognised Rats and called out, and so there was no firing. But it could have been a dangerous situation if it hadn't been for Rats barking.

'Certainly, there was always a danger having a dog along—which was why we tried to make sure he never followed us at night. You couldn't always depend on him keeping quiet—at least not during the day. Sometimes he would run into a field and bark at something. But I can't ever remember him barking at the wrong time.'

By now, Rats had taken to sleeping at the bottom of Corporal O'Neil's bed.

'I'd put him at my feet to start with, but he'd somehow work his way up during the night and when you woke in the morning, the first thing you saw was his head.' He enjoyed his meals—his favourite dish being sausages and chips—and apart from the gash in his stomach, always appeared very healthy.

He also found himself a new chum—'a wee white dog called Scruffy. But he always played with this dog outside the camp. He never attempted to bring Scruffy inside.'

Outside the camp, Rats half-strutted, half-waddled his way through the hungry pack of stray dogs that gathered there daily.

'He didn't so much order them about as dominate them by sheer personality.'

The sight of Rats bossing big dogs around struck O'Neil as one of the funniest things he had ever seen in his life.

'I mean, I nicknamed him "The Bravest Midget"—the sight of him at four feet nothing (in human terms) bossing six-footers around was something you had to see.'

On the whole, the townspeople ignored him.

'Oh, I remember one night, a civilian tried to give him the boot, but the Jock in command told the guy to beat it—and that was that.'

O'Neil was not too worried by the attitude of the locals.

'We knew we were there as policemen—and that was good enough for us. When you served in other places, you met with friendliness, cups of tea and that sort of thing, but never in Crossmaglen. No one would talk to us. They were very bitter towards the troops. The most one ever got was a nasty or sly remark as they passed us. I accepted that. But the worst thing was that you had to watch some of your own young guys in case they got nasty in return, and then you'd get a comeback from higher up. If somebody is abusive or something like that, it can take an awful lot of willpower to hold back. One of our jobs was to check the pubs regularly and they never even talked to us, just ignored us. Even the barmen ignored us.

'One of their tricks in a pub was to pass jeering remarks about us in Gaelic. One of our chaps was a Highlander, however, who spoke Scottish Gaelic himself. You should have seen their faces when he started answering them back! I found that if you kept your cool and didn't try to retaliate, then it annoyed them. They wanted to provoke you, that was all.

'But I do want to make it clear, my experiences there have not put me off Irish people in any way. I have a lot of Irish friends and I know that Crossmaglen was a special place. Most of the people would have been friendly enough if it hadn't been that they feared the IRA.'

Corporal O'Neil's views, added to his understanding and tolerance, are all the more marked when it is remembered that his regiment lost five men during this tour. One was killed in Crossmaglen Square when a remotely controlled bomb exploded in a derelict building as a patrol passed; two lost their lives in a helicopter accident, and two more died in the Warrenpoint massacre of eighteen

British troops which coincided with the murder of Lord Mountbatten.

That summer a BBC TV crew arrived to make a brief film about the life of the troops 'in the front line' and, in the course of their visit, they discovered Rats.

And as a result, Rats became something of a TV star. The little dog's warmth and personality, his ability to merit newspaper headlines or appearances on TV, made the Company more aware than ever of the valuable boost he was giving to the troops' morale.

In his honour, therefore, a special medal was struck and he was formally given an army number. The medal, made from a dog-disc, had the Queen's head on one side, and the legend 'Rats. Delta 777'—Delta for Delta Company, 777 because three sevens were considered lucky—on the other side. Along with the medal went a red and white ribbon with his 'army number' on it.

Rats received his medal at a special ceremony. The entire Company paraded outside the walls of their Submarine while a piper played 'Scotland the Brave' and other Highland airs, and the company sergeant major pinned the medal on the dog-collar of the army's most unusual recruit. The medal was later removed and hung on the board at the entrance to the base for all to see, before being later taken to HQ at Bessbrook to be placed among other mementoes of the Army's stay in Crossmaglen.

For Corporal O'Neil, Rats' new-found fame proved a mixed blessing. His two sons, young Joseph (aged five) and Kevin (aged three) had seen what they called 'daddy's dog' on TV 'and nothing would do but that I would promise to bring him back to Glasgow. I had a terrible time explaining to them that I couldn't do that—

so I had to promise them their own pup instead.'

Next to questions about Nadine, Rats took up much of the time that O'Neil spent chatting on the telephone with his family. 'And, of course, I had to send several photographs home.'

A sad moment came for him when the time arrived for the Queen's Own Highlanders to leave Crossmaglen, handing over to the Prince of Wales Company, 1st Battalion, Welsh Guards.

'I asked Corporal Arwel Lewis of the Welsh Guards if he would be prepared to look after Rats, and he agreed that he would. So he did patrols with me for a few days, getting to know the dog in the way I had. I felt pretty angry that I wasn't allowed to take Rats with me—and a lot of the other chaps felt the same way. Some of them urged me, "Go on, take him in your kitbag and to hell with it!" but I had been warned that I was to do no such thing.'

Rats, of course, sensed that the QOH were about to leave and that he was not going with them.

'When he saw all the cases and kit being loaded aboard the helicopter he realised it was happening to him again,' recalls Corporal O'Neil. 'You know, I don't think anybody has realised how much and how often Rats must have been hurt in his lifetime. I'm not talking now about his physical injuries, but the way he struck up so many close friendships and then saw his friends leave him, without knowing why or where they were going.

'If a dog has any mind at all, he must have been badly hurt, for he had to keep finding a new friend all the time. He was prepared to stick to a man. But no man ever stuck to him—not permanently, that is. So he gave out all the love and affection he had—and then his master would disappear, and he would be left to find somebody else to whom he could give his affection.'

On this occasion, Rats travelled up to Bessbrook, thus avoiding the poignancy of another Crossmaglen farewell.

'He just jumped into the helicopter and sat, as usual, beneath my seat. But at Bessbrook, it was very, very sad. Rats had cried when the corporal I had taken him from went away, and now he cried again. It's a strange and disturbing thing to see a dog cry—whining miserably. I was crying myself, of course, and doing my best not to let anybody see. Then we jumped into the back of the army lorry and off we drove. Corporal Lewis, who had come up to Bessbrook specially, had to lift Rats in his arms and hold him there as he struggled to follow us. And that's the last I ever saw of Rats—that little face peeping up above the arms of the corporal. I just kept waving until we were out of sight.'

To Corporal O'Neil his friendship with Rats 'still seems like a fairy-tale'.

Rats, he thought, had given every soldier in Crossmaglen something that they would always value; they could never forget him.

'I think everybody else thought I was a bit batty the way I used to talk to Rats—but, you know, he was almost like a human being to me.'

Why Rats, though? Why not Fleabus or Nutter or some other dog? Surely he was just a cross-breed, a mongrel? What made Rats so especially attractive?

'I think it was because he *was* so scruffy that he became the soldiers' dog he did. A pedigree dog would have been no good in those circumstances. Rats was a dog who could be a normal soldier's dog. When a chap returns from a

81

patrol, he isn't neat and tidy—so he doesn't want a posh dog.

'Rats was often filthy and dirty, of course—he couldn't be anything else in all that mud. I washed or showered him about once a week, although he hated it. As soon as he knew he was going into the water, he was off—whoosh!

'Sometimes I'd have to do it two or three times a week. When he was washed, though, he looked completely different, really lovely. He was pure white on the toes and under the stomach and the rest was a brownish, rusty colour. To me anyway,' said Joseph O'Neil, 'he'll always be a small legend.'

SIX

The first time Major Vyvyan Harmsworth, MVO, saw Rats was when the 1st Battalion, Welsh Guards, were undergoing special training in Britain for their forthcoming tour in Northern Ireland.

One evening, a Grenadier Guards officer produced a photograph, showing the Grenadier Company who had served there lined up like a football team. Right in the middle, clasped in the arms of Captain Bolitho, was a little corgi-like dog.

'When you get there,' the officer said to Major Harmsworth, 'be a good chap and for God's sake look after that little fellow.'

'Who the hell is he?' inquired Harmsworth, slightly nonplussed.

'Rats. A marvellous little dog.'

'But—why?'

'Well, he's a kind of mascot.'

'A mascot? Good heavens.'

Harmsworth never forgot the injunction, however—and even if he had attempted to, events—and Rats—soon conspired to prevent him doing so.

He was sitting in his office at Battalion HQ in Bessbrook on his first day of duty busy answering Press inquiries, when a letter from the Pro-Dogs organisation in London appeared on his desk. Pro-Dogs is a group of dog-lovers and others who are concerned with canine welfare. They had heard about Rats from articles about him in newspapers and from his television appearances, and wondered whether, in view of his exploits, he might not qualify for their distinguished Gold Medal—the dog equivalent of the VC?

Harmsworth did not have much time to consider what should be done about the proposal. He had only been at his desk a few hours after his QOH colleague had moved out—before the subject of the letter abruptly presented himself, having, as it appeared, illegally boarded a helicopter.

By rights, Rats should have stayed behind in Crossmaglen, but as Harmsworth was to find out in the course of the next few weeks, 'by rights' had little meaning when it came to this small dog that had served longer in Crossmaglen than any other member of the British Army. He tended to make his own rules—when it suited him.

Nevertheless, Rats was not so undisciplined as that may sound and, indeed, he rarely boarded a helicopter without following the proper drill. When troops were about to board, he waited patiently until the air-load master, who sat in the back, gave the thumbs-up signal—meaning 'OK to board, lads.' then Rats would make a spectacular leap—having regard to his size, a jump of almost Olympic standards—on to the first step. Then he reached the second and would go bump, bump, into the aircraft, scampering down to the back where he crouched under his favourite seat. No one can remember if he adopted the proper procedures or not when the QOH moved out. Certainly Corporal O'Neil did not encourage him and what appears to have happened is that he slipped aboard, determined to follow O'Neil.

As is usual when one regiment hands over to another, the Commanding Officers meet at Bessbrook and shake hands to mark the hand-over, and this is invariably photographed by a member of the staff of *Vizor*, an army newspaper published in Belfast.

To Major Harmsworth's astonishment, in the middle of these proceedings, on this occasion, Rats padded straight into the centre of the picture.

By this time, his absence had been noted at Crossmaglen, and Corporal Lewis was on his way with strict orders to apprehend the deserter and bring him back to camp. As luck would have it, Lewis arrived just in time to be photographed 'formally' taking possession of Rats from Corporal O'Neil.

Arwel Lewis was the son of a farmer from outside Bangor, North Wales, and was not particularly interested in dogs. There were several on the farm, and they were treated as working dogs, not pets. He obtained the job of looking after Rats, so he says, 'mainly because I was an NCO and my platoon was bunking in Corporal O'Neil's room'. Nevertheless, he very soon grew extremely fond of the little dog 'and he certainly did take your mind off what was going on around you'.

Major Angus Wall, the 34-year-old Company Commander, had personally ordered Lewis to seize the dog and return him before somebody suggested a courtmartial. Angus Wall, born in Cheshire—and for recruiting purposes, parts of Cheshire, as a border county, are considered part of the Principality—was now on his fourth tour of Northern Ireland. This was his first experience as a Company Commander there, however, although he had previously served as Company Commander with United Nations forces in Cyprus.

'That was a very different scene, though, very pleasant. Not the same at all as Crossmaglen, where you often went out with a fair certainty that you weren't all going to come back.'

Major Wall was extremely tall—almost six and a half feet in height—and a fine rugby forward. With his Company Sergeant Major, William Evans, he had played a considerable part in the success of the Welsh Guards rugby team, which the CSM still coaches.

He quickly noted Rats' personality, and recognised the good effect he could have on the men.

'You are always aware of this strange thing, this affinity, that soldiers have towards children and animals. I was certainly very much prepared to encourage the idea of having Rats in the Company, once I was satisfied that he wouldn't interfere with military duties.

'In fact, there were several dogs wandering around outside the base and part of the trouble was, of course, that you never knew whether they belonged to anybody or not. There was one called Scruff, which the Guardsmen rather liked, and which tried to do as Rats did, and attach himself to patrols, and then in that way tried to get into the camp.

'There were several others, too, all trying to come in with the patrols. But my good CSM Evans, who in many respects was responsible for keeping the place clean and tidy, quite rightly removed them—and not always too gently, because things could otherwise have got out of hand. We could easily have had a pack of dogs living in the camp—with all the health hazards that this would mean, so I wasn't prepared to allow any more in apart from Rats.'

Major Wall had first noticed Rats when he spent five days in the base during the summer, familiarising himself with the scene.

'You could see at once that he was quite a character. He was perky and often had very good expressions on his face, and I noticed him getting frightfully excited when he knew a helicopter was coming . . .'

Rats, of course, would start to run around the helipad long before any of his human colleagues knew the aircraft was coming, picking up the noise of its engines literally minutes before it was discernible to human ears.

On return from Bessbrook, Corporal Lewis made sure that Rats was tucked up safely in a bunk, after he had eaten his usual evening meal. The army cooks had already discovered Rats' meal-times, and they had provided him with chicken, one of his favourite dishes. A day or so later, Lewis moved into a six-man bunk room reserved for NCOs, but Rats stayed on in the big dormitory under the immediate charge of two Guardsmen, Phillips and Webber.

Within a week he had ceased to pine and was following Corporal Lewis eagerly on patrols. 'He had his own patrol of dogs by this time, so, in effect, there would be two patrols out at the same time. A platoon of Welsh Guards, and at the head of them another platoon of dogs—led by Rats! He did a lot for us on patrol, which could be grim enough knowing that something might happen at any moment. He gave a bit of humour and "humanity" to a patrol, which we all appreciated . . .'

To Major Harmsworth the situation in Crossmaglen was never less than bizarre.

Here, young soldiers, many of them not much more than 18, were continually being airlifted into what he described as 'this bloody awful place, where one in six of the soldiers killed in action had died. Many felt lonely or oppressed by the tension and sense of dread, but when they walked into the camp and saw Rats, and realised that he had been bombed, blasted and shot at, and yet was still asleep and apparently unconcerned, that made them think, "Well, if *he* can survive, then there's a chance for me." I think that for many of our young Welsh Guardsmen, Rats was more than just a dog, he was a symbol of survival.'

The tension was no less tangible because the soldiers rarely showed it. When Major Harmsworth brought visiting newspapermen or TV crews there, 'you'd go into the barrack rooms and find people playing cards, being very jolly, writing letters to their girl friends, or discussing family problems at home. It wasn't until something happened that you realised how the tension had been there all the time. I remember once taking an American journalist around the base and the town, and he summed it all up very graphically by saying: "This place is as mean as cat shit." '

It was certainly one thing to order young soldiers to advance towards an enemy behind a screen of tanks, as had often been done in the Second World War; it was altogether another to ask two men perhaps to go into a house to check whether it contained explosives, which they knew could be detonated by radio from a distance of metres or even kilometres away, while they were inside.

They might examine the house, and then come out and tell the Bomb Disposal Squad: 'There's a box sitting in the corner of the kitchen, and it's got red wires coming from the top and green wires from the bottom.'

Under those circumstances, men had not only to be brave; they had to stay cool and calm as well. They could not afford to get excited or to show their real feelings, or attempt to dispel their inner fears by some rash act of heroism—or folly—that in a more conventional battle might have earned them a medal. Even on patrol, when fears were to some extent dispelled by the sheer physical activity involved, the young soldiers had to think positively. While they were cautious, they could never show any apprehension they felt, but had always to appear confident and in command of events.

The weirdness of the Crossmaglen base itself added to the general feeling of the abnormal that made such an impression on Major Harmsworth. A Royal Ulster Constabulary station—'barracks' in local parlance—was a constant target of attack, and manned by policemen doing twenty-four-hour stints at a time. In the yard or open space beside it was the compound, surrounded by corrugated iron fencing and barbed wire. Inside this was where the troops lived. The area was so vulnerable to attack that virtually everything was brought in by helicopter.

'There was what we called the nine o'clock shuttle— although the time varied every day to confuse the Opposition,' explains Major Harmsworth. 'You'd jump on and find the most extraordinary collection of people aboard. One morning, a carpenter with his bag of tools. Next, a plumber or somebody else. There was always building or fixing going on. Only when really heavy materials had to be moved into camp would a convoy of army vehicles be sent down. Local carpenters and plumbers and other workmen, of course, would not have gone into the camp by road. They did not want to be seen, for obvious reasons. It was all a kind of Alamo situation, really. You had all these people going in every morning, with mail, food, rations and other stuff for the 120 men in the base carried in a net slung under the helicopter. Then the aircraft would move out with perhaps dustbins or other rubbish in their place.'

Helicopters, of course, were to the army what buses are to civilians. Up to fifty regular flights a day in the Armagh area were controlled by 'Buzzards'—an army acronym for air traffic controllers. The helicopters shuttled from Battalion HQ to outbases in the frontline area. In addition, there were unscheduled flights when generals or civilian specialists might be flown in. The military use of helicopters varied. Some undertook routine aerial patrols to see what the Opposition was up to; others dropped foot patrols in the countryside, and picked them up next day, or left them out near the border for a day or so with instructions to find their own way back, checking and searching as they went. For Rats, with his passion for helicopters, all this activity was sheer delight.

'He'd get into a definite muddle at times,' says Major Harmsworth, 'because he'd simply jump into any helicopter that arrived when he was in the mood. He would have no idea where that particular helicopter was going, of course. It could go to any one of six locations—or even right back to Belfast.

'When this sort of thing happened, he'd often arrive

somewhere that was closing down for the night, and so he would be put up in the Officers' Mess. Then, next morning, some compassionate type would say: "OK, Rats, we'll take you home again." If he had been up in Belfast, which was sixty miles away, they'd bring him to Bessbrook, and then he'd change helicopters there and come on back to base.

'If you saw him at any location other than Crossmaglen, he'd usually be sitting near the helicopter pad, shivering in the cold, perhaps, waiting for his helicopter to arrive. Then somebody would say: "Rats, that's *your* helicopter," and he'd leap aboard.

'If it weren't the right one, he'd just sit there until he was given the order to leave. It was obvious, sometimes, that he had lost himself completely and needed a bit of help to get back to base, and so he'd wait patiently until somebody said, "Right, Rats, that's *your* one. Crossmaglen," and point towards it. Then he'd be off.

'I don't think one could claim he ever actually knew when he was arriving at Crossmaglen, though I've always *suspected* he did. He could certainly tell, by the change in engine tone, when the machine was about to land. At that point he would creep out from beneath the seat at the back, where he had spent the journey, and move forward near the door. He was always eager to jump off. It's very difficult to judge height from the ground accurately, even for humans. I imagine it must have been almost impossible for him. I don't believe he could tell whether the helicopter was four feet off the ground, or thirty.

'Some pilots have sworn to me that they saw him jump out of helicopters from thirty feet—simply because he had made a misjudgement. They used to say they almost had heart attacks sitting at the front and seeing this dog suddenly fly out on all fours.

'Fortunately, the Armagh countryside is very boggy and so the worst thing that ever happened to Rats was that he ended up with an almighty bang to his body that certainly couldn't have done him any good. I personally can vouch that he's jumped out from seven or eight feet for I've seen him do it. When you think of all the bombs, bullets, and these free-fall parachute drops without any parachute that he has endured, and when you consider that he isn't much bigger than a rabbit, I can't think of any soldier who has survived as much as he has and still lived.'

Sergeant Joseph Holland, from Swansea, was based at Battalion HQ in Bessbrook, and as a result came to know Rats almost as well as his fellow-Guardsmen cooped up in Crossmaglen.

'He'd often come up on the morning helicopter and stay with us until another one went back in the evening,' he recalls. 'He might arrive at any time, and if he turned up on a late flight, we'd find him a bed to sleep somewhere, and he'd stay over for breakfast and catch the next flight back. I was given the job of looking after him at Bessbrook, although to be honest, he was well able to take care of himself most of the time. He'd often nearly give me heart failure, all the same. As a helicopter came in, I'd see him standing in the doorway, without harness, and he'd be still twenty or thirty feet off the ground.

'It was sometimes difficult to control him, when it came to helicopters. Usually, he was very good, but sometimes he'd anticipate orders or mix them up and jump aboard one he shouldn't have boarded. I remember once, he got away from me and leaped aboard a helicopter which was taking a unit out on a four-day patrol. I made a grab for him—but couldn't risk going any farther as the rotary blades had started. The trouble was that we had an important Press party coming that day specially to see him—so we had a heck of a job sending *another* helicopter after him to take him back!'

Signals were constantly arriving from Crossmaglen: 'RATS ARRIVING YOUR DESTINATION FIVE MINUTES STOP TURN HIM AROUND GIVE HIM KICK UP BACKSIDE AND SEND HIM BACK STOP'.

The little dog had no hesitation in joining patrols while waiting at Bessbrook.

'I remember once when he came up to see us,' says Sergeant Holland, 'we were patrolling a housing estate where every dog there is trained to attack *anything* in army green.

'Three or four big dogs made for us, but Rats stood his ground, and although only up to their knees in size, he attacked them *and* routed them. He was useful in many other ways, too. When we were crossing fields, for instance, he would go through the bushes first, and if there had been anybody there waiting for us, Rats would have found him first.

'He used to sum up situations for us. He'd stop, his ears would prick up and his tail would rise, and we'd see him listening and sniffing. Any hedge we came to, he'd run up and down it several times to make sure the way was clear for us before going through.

'Personally, I even used Rats to get my breakfast sometimes! At Bessbrook we'd have to work all the hours God sent and so would maybe sleep on in the mornings and miss breakfast. If Rats had come up, I'd walk in late and tell the cook: "Dog's breakfast", and without a word I'd be handed a dozen sausages and a couple of eggs. So I'd slip Rats three or four sausages and eat the rest—therefore I was often grateful for his presence!

'He'd sometimes arrive when we were least expecting him—depending on where he had been, and whether he had got lost, or whatever. We'd be in bed at maybe four or five o'clock in the morning and a helicopter would arrive, and the next thing we knew, Rats was in the room and licking my hand. He was as smart as hell. He could come in through the swing door without any trouble, and he even learned how to paw the handle of the outer door to open it. And he was very well behaved so far as toilets went—at least when at Bessbrook. I watched him several times get up from his place under my bed, push open the swing door, work the handle of the outside door and go outside and then come back in quietly, and curl up where he'd been.

'As for our wives, well, once he became a TV star and began to have his name in the papers, all the women became tremendously interested in him. Whenever we spoke to our wives on the phone or had a letter from home, there was always a lot of talk about Rats. Later, when he became ill and I became even more involved with him, I remember telling my wife: "You know, some of you women are more concerned about that dog than you are about your own husbands!" I meant that half-jokingly, of course, but they did seem to care about him. I think, honestly, it helped them to take their minds off our problems. I know it helped my wife Wendy in that way . . .'

Back in Crossmaglen, subtle changes were taking place in the relationship between the army and the local population—and some of the changes could be put down to Rats and his growing fame. Not all of them, unfortunately, were to Rats' personal advantage. His survival suddenly became a matter of concern.

'Crossmaglen originated as a tinkers' village,' says Major Harmsworth. 'It's placed at the junction of six roads, some of them leading into Southern Ireland, and it has the most curious atmosphere imaginable. Today, such is the tension, fear and even resentment, that most people there will not talk to strangers even if they are civilian. I've known visiting Americans or Germans try to start a conversation with the locals and still get completely ignored.

'One American, I remember, whose people had originally come from that part of the world, tried to strike up a conversation with one local but as soon as he opened his mouth, he was told to "F— off!" It's like walking about in a town of ghosts—shadowy people totally ignoring you, never talking.'

As Company Sergeant Major Evans puts it, 'It was like being stationed in Sicily. Nobody would talk—mainly because they're frightened. The law of *omerta*—silence— rules in Crossmaglen.

'In fact, you can talk to a lot of Catholics who themselves have never liked going near Crossmaglen, even in normal times. There's a saying apparently, "There are more roads than honest men in Crossmaglen." Sometimes it is said that perhaps Crossmaglen ought to be in Southern Ireland, in the Republic. But I think some of the population would go bananas if that ever happened! They're smugglers—and that would be the worst thing that could ever happen to them.

'I'm not saying that it's in any way dangerous to go there—provided, that is, you're not connected with the army or with the security forces. But you'd be mad to go—because you'd be certain to be treated with suspicion and hostility. Everybody is carefully checked. They know every foreigner, and you mightn't even be served a drink in a pub if they thought you didn't measure up.'

Yet, as the tour of the Welsh Guards continued, there seemed to be a slight softening in attitude.

'They're Celts and we're Celts,' says Company Sergeant Major Evans, 'and I believe that helped a lot.'

Two Guardsmen, Simon Skinner from Cardiff, and Alan Douglas from the Rhondda Valley, both agree.

'Initially, there was a lot of tension when we arrived. We were all tensed up, and when we saw bullet marks and bomb marks all over the place, that didn't help very much. But once we got out on the streets and came to know the people by sight and the area, then I think we began to understand the mood of the place and things started to change. You know you've a job to do—and when you start doing that, well, your attitude changes.

'By the time we arrived there, the locals had become used to the army sometimes giving them trouble—but they knew we had a job to do and more or less accepted the interference to their normal way of going about things. And the army presence in Crossmaglen was certainly very obvious. Wherever one looked, there seemed to be a Sarry-can or an observation post, or a patrol of some sort. The locals just shrugged this off or ignored us most of the time.

'When we checked in the pubs, they would never talk,

not unless you demanded an answer to a specific question such as: "Where were you on Monday night?" or something like that—where a refusal might have led to their arrest or something.

'Mind you, it was part of our job to be as friendly as possible to them—and we had orders not to hassle people. After a while, in fact, this did seem to pay off. At night, some locals might actually talk to us, even if it was only to pass a friendly remark.'

As Guardsman Skinner remembers it, 'I was never so astonished as on New Year's Eve that year. I was out patrolling in the town and a rather elderly woman came over to me and kissed me on the cheek and said, "God bless you, son. Take care." I'll never forget it.'

Rats played his part, if only a small part, in this slight relaxation of tension between the locals and the army. Once he had appeared on TV, and pictures of him had begun to appear in newspapers, a genuine interest in his doings was generated among the locals, particularly among children.

'There's Rats,' the children would shout, and there would be considerable excitement if a car full of children were stopped at a VCP and Rats was seen to be doing his favourite act of biting the tyres.

'But having a pet like that was leaving yourself a bit open,' says CSM Evans, an enormous figure of a man who gave up coal-mining to join the Guards. ('I gave up mining because I wanted to play rugby,' he insists.) He had served in Crossmaglen on an earlier tour, when things had been considerably quieter—and more serious up in Belfast—and he had a healthy regard for the way in which the locals gathered information.

'The first thing they said when I walked into one of the local pubs was: "Oh, so *you're* back, are you?" They never miss a trick.'

Whatever his experience though, CSM Evans remained well disposed towards the Irish.

'As I say, we're Celts and they're Celts, and I know Ireland well and how friendly Irish people can really be. Before the troubles, you see, I used to go to Lansdowne Road every two years to see Wales play Ireland at rugby—and we always had a marvellous time. So, to me, the overriding feeling I had in Crossmaglen was how sad it all was—how tragic that there should be any kind of Irishman trying to harm us.'

Yet Rats, for all the balance of a positive nature in his favour, was also a kind of hostage to fortune.

'I was always afraid that he might come over the fence one night—either dead or badly mutilated,' says CSM Evans. 'You had to expect that kind of mentality, for the Opposition knew how damaging such a thing could have been to the men—and there were previous cases where other army dogs had been killed or tortured—I don't mean in Crossmaglen. So I wasn't keen for that reason.

'That was one reason—apart from what Major Wall says about hygiene, which was the overriding reason—why I didn't allow other dogs in. It's a very difficult problem, you know. A soldier can take a heck of a lot—but there is a limit. So I thought it was my duty to prevent relationships becoming too personal with other dogs. We could handle Rats, more or less. But that was as far as I wanted it to go. Both the CO and I had this feeling.'

'My view,' says Sergeant Holland, 'is that some people in Crossmaglen would have turned Rats into a pair of slippers if they could have got away with it. In fact, he was kicked quite a few times. But it was a matter of the hard core, you know, and I think the publicity made them worse, and so the situation became more dangerous in that sense.

'Some of the soldiers certainly no longer wanted him out on patrol with them. They claimed that the IRA intended to kill him and were just waiting for the dog and "would kill us with him". Certainly, this would have been a tremendous boost for the IRA morale and you know the way they like publicity, and as I understand it, shots were fired at him.'

Guardsmen Skinner and Douglas do not doubt that Rats' new-found TV stardom was a double-edged weapon.

'The story we heard was that the IRA had put out a contract on him,' says Guardsman Skinner. 'They called him "soldiers' friend" and it would have upset us all badly if anything had happened to the little dog.'

'Yet we had all the children pointing at him excitedly and calling out with delight: "That's Rats! That's Rats!"' says Guardsman Douglas.

Meanwhile, the object of the fuss remained as perky and ebullient as ever.

'He slept in this big eighteen-man room,' says Guardsman Skinner, 'and he could be a right nuisance at times. I mean, he used to piss on your bed, sometimes. Everybody put up with it, of course. All you did, in fact, was put down a plastic sheet.'

'He was a pretty good dog most of the time though,' Guardsman Douglas points out. 'I mean, he didn't have much call to pee in the dormitory, for there was always a patrol going out. Patrols went out throughout the twenty-four hours at fifteen-minute intervals, and Guardsman Webber, who was one of the chaps who looked after him, had him fairly well under control, so that Rats would usually stand at the door if he wanted to go out, and then he'd disappear and maybe go through a hole in the fence and do his stuff and then come back in. But it did happen sometimes that things went wrong, particularly after he became ill.'

There was a long way to go, however, before the seriousness of Rats' condition became obvious. Looking back, those who knew him well find it almost impossible to imagine how Rats managed to display such a courageous and cheerful front for so long.

'He was always perky and ready to go right to the last. If you felt at all depressed, then he'd certainly cheer you up. You might get up in the morning feeling "Oh, not another bloody awful day", and then there would be Rats, sunny as ever, and it would cheer you up. And all this after he himself had been out patrolling for maybe half the day and half the night.'

'Other dogs went into Crossmaglen,' recalls Sergeant Holland, 'took what they could get, made a mess in the camp and then disappeared—but not Rats. Rats stuck to the troops and never dodged any of his duties. That's why he became so important. Other dogs might go down the road with a patrol for two or three hundred yards and then run off somewhere. But Rats always stuck with his patrol. He stuck with the men, and so the men stuck with him.'

Rats continued to eat normally and showed no signs of going off his food.

'During his service, he must have dealt with about

twenty cooks,' says Major Harmsworth. 'Half of them liked him, and so he had all the best bits of meat from them. The other half didn't like a dog in the kitchen under any circumstances, they considered it unhygienic, so Rats got booted out. His favourite dish, as I remember it, was NAAFI steak pie.'

'He got exactly the same number of meals a day as I did, and the same sort of food,' says Guardsman Kevin Webber, a native of Barry, South Glamorgan.

'Three meals a day, and if there was only one steak left, then he always had that. I thought the world of that little dog. He was always loyal and cheerful and never seemed down in the dumps—at least not until he became sick. He would always stay close to the patrols—and he always stuck close to Corporal Lewis until the Corporal left the army. He was always at his heels before that, and always at mine after Corporal Lewis left. I can only say that he was a marvellous little dog.'

In fact, it soon began to seem that not only Crossmaglen, but half Britain, had developed a deep admiration for Rats and for his qualities of character and devotion to duty. More than once, Corporal Lewis had to take him up to Belfast in a helicopter so that he could make a guest appearance on a TV programme.

And then, just before Christmas, big news arrived in Crossmaglen. Rats, it appeared, had been awarded the Pro-Dogs Gold Medal as Dog of the Year, the citation being 'For Valour and Devotion to Duty,' and he was to go to London to receive his decoration.

SEVEN

On December 9, 1979, Rats travelled to London in the baggage compartment of a scheduled flight from Belfast. With him came Corporal Lewis, who on landing took Rats to the BBC studios at Lime Grove, where he was interviewed on the family programme, 'Nationwide'.

Corporal Lewis then took him to the awards dinner and ball being held by Pro-Dogs in north-west London. Pro-Dogs is a national charity dedicated to promoting the interest of dogs. It has a panel of consultants, doctors, vets, and other experts who advise on various matters affecting dogs, their owners and the general public.

Rats was only one of a number of distinguished dogs present on this occasion. Many had previously won prizes at Cruft's and other dog shows, and now arrived to claim awards as diverse as life-saving or for making an exceptional contribution as a family pet. All were highly groomed and of impeccable pedigree.

As the winners of the various awards arrived with their owners, a soldier was seen leading what was clearly a little mongrel along the pavement. A Cruft's show judge turned to his companion and said, 'Well, there's *one* that won't be going.' He was quite wrong, for Rats became the star of the show.

During the evening, kennel maids from Battersea Dogs' Home looked after the dogs on special benches. The show dogs were used to this, but Rats was not. Show benches, he decided, were no place for an active army dog. He wanted to be where the action was, and insisted on taking his place with Corporal Lewis at the dining table. Here he joined in the proceedings with enthusiasm and great gusto.

When everyone clapped when the winners in various categories came forward to receive their awards, Rats showed his approval by barking his applause.

Then Mrs Lesley Scott Ordish, the founder of Pro-Dogs, read the citation: 'Rats: Dog of War: Delta 7/777: For bravery, devotion to duty, and the comfort you have provided to soldiers serving in Crossmaglen, Pro-Dogs is pleased to award your Gold Medal.'

When she placed the medal on a tartan ribbon around Rats' neck, Rats barked with joy. She then handed to Corporal Lewis a present for Rats—a bone biscuit wrapped in silver foil. But Rats was never one for ordinary dog food; he preferred army cooking . . .

Rats appeared as perky and cheerful as ever, and few who saw him could have suspected that the old soldier was just recovering from yet another injury, or that his health was causing concern and would soon lead to his retirement on medical grounds.

A week before he flew to London, an anxious Major Wall had telephoned Major Harmsworth at Bessbrook.

'Look,' he said, 'I'm worried about old Rats. He hasn't been out today, and I think he's a bit poorly.'

Harmsworth at once got in touch with the Army Dog Unit at Long Kesh prison camp and arranged that he should see Captain T. C. Morton, the Veterinary Officer.

'Rats came down with his handler, Corporal Lewis,' Major Harmsworth recalls, 'and I could see that he was not himself at all. I kept him overnight and then sent him up by car the following morning. It was quite a little operation, really, because it involved sending three people with him—a driver, an armed escort and someone in the back to look after him. I know that this may seem like one of those unacceptable things that make taxpayers complain. But really, from the point of view of morale at Crossmaglen alone, we had no option but to do it.'

'I dressed in civvies,' says Sergeant Holland, 'and carried a pistol in my pocket. Both the driver and escort also dressed in civvies. I took Rats into the back seat, and kept his head covered in a rug for most of the way. Every time we came to traffic lights, or any place where we had to slow down, I covered him completely with the rug. We couldn't risk him being recognised.

'It was like having a child in the car, you know, for he always got car sick. That was one of the most surprising things, really. Rats could travel anywhere by helicopter and nothing would happen, but once he was inside a car, believe it or not, he was sick.

'I sat there in the back and he would be sick all over me. But there was no way I was going to stop on a motorway and let him out or anything like that. So I waited until we reached the Maze (Long Kesh) and then cleaned myself up there. During the journey I used to say to myself: "I've got two bullets in this gun. One for Rats and one for myself if anything happens." We were really worried that there might be an attempt on him.

'His eyes were badly bloodshot on that occasion and the vet reported that he was run down and should be kept there for a couple of days.'

'In fact,' says Major Harmsworth, 'there were loads of

rats in the Crossmaglen camp and he had obviously got into a scrap with them and just as obviously he had much the worst of it. He had been badly bitten in the neck, and was suffering from blood poisoning. He was also run down—too much attention to duty, really—and had a cyst on his paw, and mites in his ear. His coat wasn't right, either. Even with the best will in the world, Crossmaglen was such a muddy and dirty place that everybody was constantly up to their knees in dirt, and Rats couldn't help but pick up his fair share.'

Ill, and with a price on his head or not, Christmas 1979 turned out to be the peak of Rats' army career. His appearances on TV and constant attention from newspapers ensured a staggering response from people all over Britain.

'Between two and three hundred letters began arriving *every day* at Bessbrook addressed personally to Rats that Christmas,' recalls Sergeant Holland. 'I reckon that the total number altogether must have amounted to several thousand—the truth is that finally there were so many we lost count. I personally answered dozens. Some came signed with a paw mark, and some I answered with Rats' signature, that is, his paw mark on them.

' "Dear Rosie, Thanks for all your good wishes, Rats", and then his paw mark. That sort of thing. Then we received parcels. Food parcels of every description, and presents of all sorts. Doggy drops, bones, rubber balls, baskets, doggy-beds, pillows—you think of it, Rats received it. We handled a lot of the stuff up at Bessbrook, for we weren't in the same situation as the lads down in Crossmaglen. But even then, they were snowed under.'

'I think it was very much to the army's credit,' says

Major Harmsworth, 'that every single letter that was written to Rats was eventually replied to. I know that one officer, on duty at Crossmaglen, in the Ops Room keeping tab on all the patrols, would answer them, one after the other, throughout the wee small hours, and lots of other people did their share as well. It was all quite amazing, really.'

'Fortunately, I didn't get involved in having to answer the letters,' says Corporal Lewis. 'I had patrols to do. But the camp was almost snowed under with letters and Christmas cards and presents. Rats received a dog-lead— and Christmas cake. And all sorts of squeaky toys—you know, made out of rubber. And he had a bean-bag, which is meant for dogs to lie down in—like a sleeping bag. It's like a pillow of soft covers. I tried to persuade Rats to sleep on it. I'd lift him up and put him down on it, but then he'd jump straight off it and climb up on my bed instead.

'He enjoyed the dog biscuits, certainly, and the choco-late drops and so on. And he was delighted with all the squeaky toys. They were made out of tough rubber, so he couldn't do them much damage. There was one toy in particular, I remember, a squeaky duck, that he really loved.

'All I had to do was to put it on the bed, tweak it a bit and then he'd attack it ferociously. He'd bite at it, jump on it and generally savage it. But the more he jumped on it, of course, the more the rubber duck squeaked—and so the more he jumped on it. It was really great fun. So far as I could see, he was trying to bite the squeak out of it.

'Rats received so many toys that we sometimes allowed his chum Scruff into the camp to join in the fun. But Scruff was not really supposed to come in—he was a filthy dog, and there was this whole question of hygiene. Anyhow, we also played a lot of ball with Rats. We'd throw a rubber ball in the air and he'd jump for it or maybe skid all over the floor, trying to catch it. He was a game little fellow all right, and he'd play with a toy until we were ready to drop ourselves.'

'He certainly loved that squeaky duck,' recalls Guardsman Webber. 'He'd go almost crazy with that. Just give it to him and he'd amuse himself for hours.'

'I remember somebody at one stage saying: "That dog is getting more Christmas cards than all of us put together," ' says Guardsman Skinner. 'This was quite true. One day, a sack arrived with Christmas cards for almost two hundred of us. But that same day Rats got *two* full sacks—all to himself.'

'Showers of letters were arriving for him all the time,' says Guardsman Douglas. 'It eventually became so bad that an officer who had started off opening the letters himself and then passing them on to whoever was available to answer finally set up a special department. That Christmas, six of us were specially detailed to deal with Rats' correspondence.

'Women, mainly, wrote to him. And children, of course. I think the children thought that perhaps he could read or something. The women, though, wrote time after time. One of them even sent him bundles of magazines—as though he could read!'

'Others sent him doggie magazines. We used to show him pictures of dogs,' says Skinner. 'But it didn't work particularly well.'

'There was one lady who lived in Norfolk,' recalls Alan Douglas. 'She used to send him a regular parcel. It always turned out to be old copies of the *Radio Times* or *TV Times*, and so was absolutely useless. I wouldn't know what she had in mind, really. I mean, he couldn't read, could he? And old *TV Times* weren't much good to us, the thing, really.

'But the *thought* was there,' Guardsman Skinner reminds him.

'Yes,' says Guardsman Douglas. 'The kind thought was the thing really.

'Then the Pioneers up at Bessbrook made him two special jackets. One was a combat jacket for use on patrols, and the other a red ceremonial jacket with the insignia of the Welsh Guards stitched on it. There was even some talk of equipping him with a bearskin, but nothing ever came of that . . .'

With Christmas over and Rats' status climbing rapidly towards that of national celebrity, it soon became clear that all was not well with him.

'We'd still see him barking and running round in circles when he heard a helicopter coming. Or we'd see him leading a bunch of strays round Crossmaglen as though he were a Field Marshal,' says Major Harmsworth. 'And certainly, there were no signs that he was slowing up in any way. I would be walking round the town with a patrol or perhaps showing a visitor around, and suddenly I'd see Rats careering wildly across the road, from one side to the other, and I'd swear he was bound to get killed by a car or something.'

'I didn't see all that much of him personally,' says Major Wall. 'As Company Commander, there were a lot of other things for me to do. But although he never personally followed me on patrol I became as fond of him as anybody else and I used to write home to my son about him and send photographs, and that sort of thing.

'I was very concerned, too, that everybody who wrote to Rats received a reply. I wouldn't say he was much use militarily to us—because he would sometimes bark when he shouldn't, so his presence could be a disadvantage. But I liked his cocky look—and the way he growled at strays and kept them from coming into camp. He always knew his position, and was determined not to surrender it.

'In the end, I think, there was a general feeling among some of the other troops serving in Northern Ireland, even among members of our own battalion serving in other stations, that we in Crossmaglen were getting far too much publicity and attention from the general public. But what could we do? It was all because of Rats.

'Towards the end, even some of the men in the camp seemed to think that Rats was perhaps receiving too much attention. That surprised me really, because the whole Company was constantly benefiting from his presence. I think we received more than our fair share of whatever goodies there were—ladies sent us some marvellous home-made cakes, and things like that. But in some extraordinary way—and I really don't know how seriously this was felt—some of the men appeared to resent the publicity he had been given.

'Certainly, his presence and the constant demands of the Press generated a lot of extra work—to which most of us, of course, were only too happy to contribute. This could be a trifle exacting at times, particularly when it involved producing Rats at inconvenient moments.

'My CSM Evans, for instance, is a really marvellous

man with a great sense of humour, and somebody who was an immense support to me personally—but I can still picture him sitting in the Operations Room, perhaps late in the evening, trying to deal with the many returns he had to send out, when there would be a telephone call from Battalion HQ. Rats had to be sent hither or yonder for the benefit of the TV or the Press. I have to say that at moments like that, CSM Evans' remarks were not always of the printable variety.'

'Some of the fellows resented him,' admits Guardsman Webber. 'You could aggravate Rats, mess around with him and he'd never even snap at you. But once or twice he must have been near doing so. A couple of people used to annoy him quite a bit. It was sheer envy, I think—they didn't like him because he was appearing on TV and they weren't. He would just avoid them, and not go near them.'

There was never any question, however, that for the vast majority of the men in the Crossmaglen base, even after the mountain of publicity he received, there were only two major concerns about Rats. The first was the question of his deteriorating health, the second of his continuing safety.

'After the publicity, there were always civilians who would try and call him away from a patrol,' says Guardsman Webber. 'I don't mean that they all had some evil intent or anything like that. Some of them may have wanted to give him the odd boot or two, but many of them, I suppose, just wanted to stroke him. He wouldn't go near a civilian, however. You had to be wearing a uniform to get near Rats. Even then, he'd only go near you if he liked you. If he didn't like you, he would show it. He would move away and just leave you. And yet he loved to be stroked. He always slept at the bottom of my bed, and I always had to make sure that I stroked him before he would go to sleep.'

There seemed little doubt, however, that there were those living in or around South Armagh who would have had no compunction about seeing Rats eliminated.

On one dark and dismal evening, as a patrol trudged through the Ulster drizzle, Rats and a small bunch of strays in attendance, a car came careering along the road towards them. As it approached, the driver suddenly swerved, and—or so it seemed to the patrol—deliberately ran over one of the strays.

'I was in the Operations Room on duty when the animal was brought in,' says CSM Evans. 'The moment I looked at him I thought he was Rats. The woman driver was brought into the police station and questioned about the incident, because we believed—and still believe—that she thought the dog was Rats, and that she deliberately ran over it.

'She maintained that she simply swerved to avoid the patrol, but our fellows insisted that she had deliberately gone over the animal. And damn me, she had, of course. It was quite deliberate and obvious that she only did it because she thought she was running over Rats.

'That was the type of mentality we were up against. That's what helped to make everything about Cross-maglen so sad.'

'Rats was a better soldier than all of us,' declares Guardsman Skinner. Yet the fact was that his presence in the camp was becoming something of a liability.

'Towards the end, he was vomiting a lot and people's tempers were getting frayed at times, although everybody realised that the little dog was ill and that it wasn't his fault,' says CSM Evans. 'Besides, to all of us, even those who resented the publicity he was receiving, there was the feeling that he was a sort of mascot. I wouldn't go so far as to say they thought he was a good-luck charm. It was correct army procedures that mattered, not good-luck charms.'

'He was sick a lot,' says Guardsman Skinner. 'He couldn't keep his food down.'

'Yet, when we went outside on patrol, there he'd be still jumping around and waiting for us and we'd feel, "Well, if *he* can do it, so can I!"' says Guardsman Douglas. 'As we went out of the camp, there he was, like a little king, with his head in the air and his tail, or what was left of it, up and a whole troop of dogs following him. He seemed then like a little king dog in his own little kingdom.'

'In a way the whole thing became almost funny,' recalls Major Wall. 'As we came to realise that Rats was ill he almost began to be given priority on helicopters, and the whole idea that he might be seriously ill and perhaps have to be taken out of action threatened to become a public relations disaster. The concern and anxiety that built up were remarkable. If Rats looked at all peaky or not quite up to things, then it at once became necessary to see that he received the best possible attention.'

But Rats was nearing the end of his service life, and X-rays taken of him at Long Kesh showed that if he had been a human being, he would long ago have been retired because of his wounds. Even so, it was not so much the damage that had been caused to him by bombs, bullets, buses and bounces from helicopters that provided the root cause of his trouble, as his unquestioning single-minded devotion to duty.

The constant patrols, the exhausting day-and-night duties he set himself, finally became too much. After all, he was no longer young, and if a year in a dog's life is equal to seven for a human being, then Rats was already in his mid-fifties, beyond the usual army retiring age. After all, only a Field Marshal *never* retires.

On February 15, 1980, after a succession of visits to the Army Dog Unit RAVC at Long Kesh, and a number of X-rays, Captain Morton wrote to Major Harmsworth:

> I am writing to you with reference to 'Rats', the dog from XMG.
>
> I have put pen to paper so that there will be no misunderstanding of any action you may take as a result of what I have to say.
>
> Having had Rats in the Veterinary Hospital a number of times, it appears to me that he becomes run down much more easily now than of yore.
>
> This is understandable in that whilst having the spirit of youth, he has an eight-year-old, well-used body. He cannot keep up the pace he used to.
>
> From a veterinary point of view I would say that his system, especially his kidneys, cannot go on taking these bouts of dehydration. Whilst they are working adequately at the moment, sooner or later, sooner if he continues at his present rate, they will become irreversibly damaged.
>
> There is also some concern about his heart in that

irregularities of rhythm and occasional murmurs have been detectable.

Adding to this the fact that he persists in chasing vehicles and is becoming slower and less adept at avoiding contact, brings me to the point of this letter.

I would ask you to seriously consider retiring Rats from active service. A permanent home wherein he can take his remaining years at a more sedentary pace would, I feel, be just reward for the contribution he has made to army morale in South Armagh.

If you wish to clarify any points I have raised, please contact me at the Dog Unit and I will endeavour to answer your questions.

The news was immediately flashed to Crossmaglen: 'Rats will not be coming back.'

As this information spread through the camp, it was clear to all that a small chapter in British Army history was about to end. In many ways it had been an extraordinary revelation of the loyalty and strong affinity that can thrive between men under stress and any animal that willingly shares their dangers.

Rats might not come back, but would continue his life elsewhere, like those with whom he had served. Events would go on for them without him and for him without them.

The situation in Crossmaglen would also continue. Other men, other units, would take over when the Welsh Guards moved out. There would also probably be other dogs at Crossmaglen, but all doubted that ever again, in terms of personality, love of soldiers and soldiering—and even in the good fortune of being in the right place at the right time—any other dog could take the place of Rats.

He had served for longer in Crossmaglen than any soldier, and as a woman admirer wrote to him from South Yorkshire: 'You deserve your rest, Rats, little hero of Ulster.'

EPILOGUE

Rats was retired to a farm in Kent where, after a strictly-controlled diet, mainly of chicken, he regained his health and learned to live and play with children in a quiet and undisturbed countryside, light-years away, it seemed, in terms of danger and discomfort, from the hardships and dangers of Crossmaglen.

Rats is happily content to pass the remainder of his days surrounded by the same affection and attention he so willingly gave to the soldiers with whom he served in Ireland. Not, of course, that he is in complete retirement; like all old soldiers, he likes to keep in touch.

He travelled to Pirbright in Surrey, for instance, for his ceremonial retirement from the army.

He appeared again on television, when Major Harmsworth stood beside him to salute the Queen Mother during the Royal Tournament at Earls Court.

He was guest of honour at a children's Christmas party to help raise funds for cardiac units at the Great Ormond Street Hospital for Sick Children. For Rats is still willing to assist a good cause, and always will be.

Back in Crossmaglen, his presence was missed— although, fortunately, his retirement came almost at the end of the Prince of Wales' Company's tour, when he would in any case have had to have been left behind, as he was on so many previous occasions when a unit moved out.

Everyone with whom he had been associated has their own especial memory of Rats. Many still keep newspaper cuttings or photographs of him in their wallets, for Rats is not a little dog to forget, but a loyal friend to remember.

'I missed him running around our feet or playing with his duck,' says Guardsman Douglas.

'I missed seeing him scrambling about, and chasing cars,' says Guardsman Skinner.

'I missed a kind, good, cheerful and loyal companion,' says Guardsman Webber.

'We still, somehow, expected to see him in the Officers' Mess, his jaws locked on a rubber ball or hanging on by his teeth as we tried to take it from him to throw it and play with him,' says Major Wall.

'I'll always remember the way he started barking or whining with excitement when a helicopter was coming in to land,' says Arwel Lewis. 'I'd have to hold him firmly on my knee or he'd be at the door, while we were still up in the air—although during the journey itself he'd be on his best behaviour, thoroughly happy and content.'

'Letters and requests for photographs still flooded in,' recalls CSM Evans. 'So far as the men were concerned, however, when he went, they had to use their common-sense. Certainly, he was missed, though. As company Sergeant Major, I had to be a bit of a disciplinarian, I'm afraid. I seemed forever to be kicking dogs out. "Take it out! Take it out!"

'After Rats went, I became a little more lenient. If there was a stray which was soaking wet, I'd let them take it in and dry it out and give it a meal. But there was a short period when it seemed that they began to collect dogs wholesale. Whenever they went out on patrol, some dog would join them, and instead of shooing it away, the patrol would allow it to follow them back to camp. The dog might end up travelling seven or eight miles.

'And then we'd have irate people coming marching up to the base demanding: "Where's my dog? So you're even kidnapping dogs now, are ye?" The men weren't stealing the dogs, of course—they were just allowing the dogs to follow them. Rats was really very badly missed, but the police advice was that dogs should be discouraged so far as possible.

'There was never any chance that any other dog would compare with Rats. Some dogs are just more affectionate than others—and Rats was a really affectionate dog. He could strike up a rapport with people, like Guardsman Webber or Guardsman Skinner. Rats was a friendly and good-natured animal and—if you like—cuddlesome. He was so small, see. I'd let him go to sleep on my lap. It was almost like having a baby in my lap.

'If I were to sum up what I think Rats meant to all of us, I'd say, "He was like an oasis of friendship in a desert of sadness." '

Rats also has his memories, and in retirement the sound of a helicopter flying overhead is still like the sound of gunfire to other old warriors. Rats will bark and circle excitedly, waiting for it to land, hoping for it to land, and, of course, it never does . . .

'An air-sea rescue helicopter flew over the other day,' says his present owner, 'and I watched his tail go up and the hairs rise, and he bounced across the lawn following it until he could go no further. I've no doubt that if it had actually landed, he'd have been straight into it.

'As it is, he's now happy to settle for cars. He hides behind a bush until I open the car door, then, before I can stop him, it's straight into the back. Fortunately, he is no longer car sick. In fact, he now loves cars and it's difficult to leave him behind when you drive off.

'My little daughter calls him Raa—and simply dotes on him. He had never known the company of children until his retirement, and she can pull his tail or tweak his nose now and he'll never complain. Rats is a very adaptable dog . . .'

Years before Rats was born—or indeed any of the soldiers with whom he served—an American essayist, Elbert Hubbard, wrote about dogs in terms that all who came in contact with Rats would instantly recognise and approve: 'The one absolutely unselfish friend who man can have in this selfish world, the one who never deserts him, the one who never proves ungrateful or treacherous is his dog.'

Perhaps, in his loyalty, his warmth of nature and his philosophical adaptability to all circumstances, including discomfort and even danger of death, Rats has a lesson all of us could learn . . .